British Railwa

LOCOI

C000055081

FIFTY-FIFTH EDITION
2013

The complete guide to all
Locomotives which operate on
the national railway network
and Eurotunnel

Robert Pritchard & Peter Hall

ISBN 978 1902 336 98 5

© 2012. Platform 5 Publishing Ltd, 3 Wyvern House, Sark Road, Sheffield, S2 4HG, England.

Printed in England by Berforts Information Press, Eynsham, Oxford.

CONTENTS

PROVISION OF INFORMATION

This book has been compiled with care to be as accurate as possible, but in some cases information is not officially available and the publisher cannot be held responsible for any errors or omissions. We would like to thank the companies and individuals which have been co-operative in supplying information to us. The authors of this series of books are always pleased to receive notification from readers of any inaccuracies readers may find in the series, to enhance future editions. Please send comments to:

Robert Pritchard, Platform 5 Publishing Ltd, 3 Wyvern House, Sark Road, Sheffield, S2 4HG, England.

e-mail: <u>robert@platform5.com</u> **Tel:** 0114 255 2625 **Fax:** 0114 255 2471

This book is updated to information received by 8 October 2012.

UPDATES

This book is updated to the Stock Changes given in **Today's Railways UK 131** (November 2012). Readers are therefore advised to update this book from the official Platform 5 Stock Changes published every month in **Today's Railways UK** magazine, starting with issue 132.

The Platform 5 magazine **Today's Railways UK** contains news and rolling stock information on the railways of Britain and Ireland and is published on the second Monday of every month. For further details of **Today's Railways UK**, please see the advertisement on the back cover of this book.

Front cover photograph: DBS-liveried 60007 "The Spirit of Tom Kendell" passes Chapel Milton with 6H03 09.47 Northwich–Tunstead on 15/09/11. **Mick Tindall**

BRITAIN'S RAILWAY SYSTEM

INFRASTRUCTURE & OPERATION

Britain's national railway infrastructure is owned by a "not for dividend" company, Network Rail (NR). Many stations and maintenance depots are leased to and operated by Train Operating Companies (TOCs), but some larger stations remain under Network Rail control. The only exception is the infrastructure on the Isle of Wight, which is nationally owned and is leased to South West Trains.

Trains are operated by TOCs over Network Rail, regulated by access agreements between the parties involved. In general, TOCs are responsible for the provision and maintenance of the locomotives, rolling stock and staff necessary for the direct operation of services, whilst NR is responsible for the provision and maintenance of the infrastructure and also for staff to regulate the operation of services.

At the time of going to press the lettering of new franchises was on hold pending a review on the franchise system ordered by the Government following the cancelling of the award of the West Coast franchise to First Group in October 2012.

DOMESTIC PASSENGER TRAIN OPERATORS

The large majority of passenger trains are operated by the TOCs on fixed-term franchises. Franchise expiry dates are shown in the list of franchisees below:

Franchise	Franchisee	Trading Name
Chiltern Railways	Deutsche Bahn (Arriva) (until 31 December 2021)	**Chiltern Railways**

Chiltern Railways operates a frequent service between London Marylebone, Banbury and Birmingham Snow Hill, with some peak services extending to Kidderminster. There are also regular services from Marylebone to Stratford-upon-Avon and to Aylesbury Vale Parkway via Amersham (along the London Underground Metropolitan Line). The fleet consists of DMUs of Classes 121 (used on the Princes Risborough–Aylesbury route), 165, 168 and 172 plus a number of loco-hauled rakes used on some of the Birmingham trains, worked by Class 67s.

Cross-Country[1]	Deutsche Bahn (Arriva) (until 11 November 2013)	**CrossCountry**

CrossCountry operates a network of long-distance services between Scotland and North-East England, also Manchester to the South West of England, Reading, Southampton, Bournemouth and Guildford, centred on Birmingham New Street. These trains are mainly formed of diesel Class 220/221 Voyagers, supplemented by a small number of HSTs on the NE–SW route. Inter-urban services also operate between Birmingham, Leicester and Stansted Airport and Nottingham, Birmingham and Cardiff. These use Class 170 DMUs.

East Midlands	Stagecoach Group plc (until 31 March 2015)	**East Midlands Trains**

EMT operates a mix of long distance high speed services on the Midland Main Line (MML), from London St Pancras to Sheffield (Leeds at peak times and some extensions to York/Scarborough) and Nottingham, and local and regional services ranging from the Norwich–Liverpool route to Nottingham–Skegness, Nottingham–Mansfield/Worksop, Nottingham–Matlock and Derby–Crewe. It also operates local services in Lincolnshire. Trains on the MML are worked by a fleet of Class 222 DMUs and ten HSTs, whilst the local and regional fleet consists of DMU Classes 153, 156 and 158.

Greater Western[2]	First Group plc (until 31 March 2013)	**First Great Western**

First Great Western operates long distance trains from London Paddington to South Wales, the West Country and Worcester and Hereford. In addition there are frequent trains along the Thames Valley corridor to Newbury and Oxford, plus local and regional trains throughout the South-West including the Cornish, Devon and Thames Valley branches, the Reading–Gatwick North Downs line and Cardiff–Portsmouth Harbour and Bristol–Weymouth regional routes. A fleet of 53 HSTs is used on the long distance trains, with DMUs of Classes 165 and 166 (and 180 from summer 2012) on the Thames Valley and North Downs work, and Classes 143, 150, 153 and 158 on local and regional trains in the South West. A small fleet of four Class 57s are maintained to work the overnight Sleeper service between London and Penzance.

Greater Anglia[3]	Abellio (until 19 July 2014)	**Greater Anglia**

Greater Anglia operates main line trains between London Liverpool Street, Ipswich and Norwich and local trains across Norfolk, Suffolk and parts of Cambridgeshire. It also runs local and commuter services into Liverpool Street from the Great Eastern (including Southend, Braintree and Clacton) and West Anglia (including Cambridge and Stansted Airport) routes. It operates a very varied fleet of Class 90s with loco-hauled Mark 3 sets, DMUs of Classes 153, 156 and 170 and EMUs of Classes 315, 317, 321, 360 and 379.

Integrated Kent	Govia Ltd (Go-Ahead/Keolis) (until 31 March 2014)	**Southeastern**

Southeastern operates all services in the South-East London suburbs, the whole of Kent and part of Sussex, which are primarily commuter services to/from London. It also operates domestic high speed trains on HS1 from St Pancras to Ashford, Ramsgate, Dover and Faversham with additional peak services on other routes. EMUs of Classes 375, 376, 465 and 466 are used, along with Class 395s on the High Speed trains.

InterCity East Coast[4]		**East Coast**

East Coast operates frequent long distance trains on the East Coast Main Line between London King's Cross, Leeds, York, Newcastle and Edinburgh, with less frequent services to Bradford, Harrogate, Skipton, Hull, Lincoln, Glasgow, Aberdeen and Inverness. A mixed fleet of Class 91s and 30 Mark 4 sets, and 14 HST sets, are used on these trains.

InterCity West Coast[5]	Virgin Rail Group Ltd. (until 8 December 2012)	**Virgin Trains**

Virgin operates long distance services along the West Coast Main Line from London Euston to Birmingham/Wolverhampton, Manchester, Liverpool and Glasgow using Class 390 Pendolino EMUs. It also operates Class 221 Voyagers between London and Chester/Holyhead, and between Birmingham and Glasgow/Edinburgh. One rake of Mark 3 loco-hauled stock is also retained and is used on an ad-hoc basis, with just one booked Euston–Crewe via Birmingham working each week.

London Rail[6]   MTR/Deutsche Bahn   **London Overground**
                                          (until 31 March 2014)

London Overground operates services on the Richmond–Stratford North London Line and the
Willesden Jn–Clapham Jn West London Line, plus the new East London Line from Highbury
& Islington to New Cross and New Cross Gate, with extensions to Crystal Palace and West
Croydon. It also runs services from London Euston to Watford Junction. All these use new
Class 378 EMUs. Class 172 DMUs are used on the Gospel Oak–Barking route.

LTS Rail   National Express Group plc   **c2c**
                                          (until 26 May 2013)

c2c operates an intensive, principally commuter, service from London Fenchurch Street to
Southend and Shoeburyness. The fleet consists entirely of Class 357 EMUs.

Merseyrail Electrics[7]   Serco/Abellio   **Merseyrail**
                                          (until 19 July 2028)

Merseyrail operates services between Liverpool and Southport, Ormskirk, Kirby, Hunts Cross,
New Brighton, West Kirby, Chester and Ellesmere Port, all worked by EMUs of Classes 507
and 508.

Northern Rail[8]   Serco/Abellio   **Northern**
                                          (until 1 April 2014)

Northern operates a range of inter-urban, commuter and rural services throughout the North
of England, including those around the cities of Leeds, Manchester, Sheffield, Liverpool and
Newcastle. The network extends from Chathill in the north to Nottingham in the south, and
Cleethorpes in the east to St Bees in the west. Longer distance services include Leeds–
Carlisle, Middlesbrough–Carlisle, Leeds–Nottingham and York–Blackpool North. The operator
uses a large fleet of DMUs of Classes 142, 144, 150, 153, 155, 156 and 158 and EMUs of
Classes 321, 322, 323 and 333.

ScotRail   First Group plc   **ScotRail**
                                          (until 8 November 2014)

ScotRail provides almost all passenger services within Scotland and also trains from Glasgow
to Carlisle via Dumfries, some of which extend to Newcastle (jointly operated with Northern).
The company also operates the overnight Caledonian Sleeper services between London and
Glasgow, Edinburgh, Inverness, Aberdeen and Fort William. In addition to the Sleeper loco-
hauled stock (hauled by Class 67s and 90s hired from DB Schenker), the company operates
a large fleet of DMUs of Classes 156, 158 and 170 and EMU Classes 314, 318, 320, 334 and
380. One loco-hauled rake is also used on a Fife Circle commuter train, hauled by a Class 67.

South Central[9]   Govia Ltd (Go-Ahead/Keolis)   **Southern**
                                          (until 25 July 2015)

Southern operates predominantly commuter services between London, Surrey and Sussex,
as well as services along the South Coast between Southampton, Brighton, Hastings and
Ashford, and also the cross-London service from South Croydon to Milton Keynes. It also
operates metro services in South London, and Gatwick Express, which is a premium non-stop
service between London Victoria and Gatwick Airport. Class 171 DMUs are used on Brighton–
Ashford and London Bridge–Uckfield services, whilst all other services are in the hands of
EMUs of Classes 313, 377, 442, 455 and 456.

South Western[10]   Stagecoach Group plc   **South West Trains**
(until 3 February 2014)

South West Trains operates trains from London Waterloo to destinations across the South and South West including Woking, Basingstoke, Southampton, Portsmouth, Salisbury, Exeter, Reading and Weymouth. It also runs services between Ryde and Shanklin on the Isle of Wight, using former London Underground 1938 stock (Class 483). The rest of the fleet comprises of DMUs Classes 158 and 159 and EMUs Classes 444, 450, 455 and 458.

Thameslink/Great Northern[11]   First Group plc   **First Capital Connect**
(until September 2013)

First Capital Connect operates trains on the Thameslink route between Bedford and Brighton via central London and the Sutton and Wimbledon loop. A joint service with Southeastern is also operated to Sevenoaks, Orpington and Ashford. FCC also runs services on the Great Northern route between London King's Cross and Moorgate to Welwyn Garden City, Hertford North, Peterborough, Cambridge and Kings Lynn. The fleet consists of EMU Classes 319 and 377 for Thameslink route services and Classes 313, 317, 321 and 365 for Great Northern route services.

Trans-Pennine Express[12]   First Group/Keolis   **TransPennine Express**
(until 1 April 2014)

TransPennine Express operates predominantly long distance inter-urban services linking major cities across the North of England, along with Edinburgh and Glasgow in Scotland. The main services are Manchester Airport/Manchester Piccadilly–Newcastle/Middlesbrough/Hull plus Liverpool–Scarborough along the North Trans-Pennine route via Huddersfield, Leeds and York, and Manchester Airport–Cleethorpes along the South Trans-Pennine route via Sheffield. It also operates Manchester Airport–Blackpool/Barrow/Windermere/Edinburgh/Glasgow. The fleet consists of DMU Classes 170 (mainly used on the Hull route) and 185.

Wales & Borders   Deutsche Bahn (Arriva)   **Arriva Trains Wales**
(until 6 December 2018)

Arriva Trains Wales operates a mix of long distance, regional and local services throughout Wales, including the Valley Lines network of lines around Cardiff, and also through services to the English border counties and to Manchester and Birmingham. The fleet consists of DMUs of Classes 121 (used on the Cardiff Bay branch), 142, 143, 150, 158 and 175 and one loco-hauled rake used on the Cardiff–Holyhead route, hauled by a Class 67.

West Midlands[13]   Govia Ltd (Go-Ahead/Keolis)   **London Midland**
(until 11 November 2013)

London Midland operates long distance/regional services from London Euston to Northampton and Birmingham/Crewe and also between Birmingham and Liverpool as well as local and regional services around Birmingham, including to Stratford-upon-Avon, Worcester, Redditch and Shrewsbury. It also operates the Bedford–Bletchley and Watford Jn–St Albans Abbey branches. The fleet consists of DMU Classes 150, 153, 170 and 172 and EMU Classes 321, 323 and 350.

Notes on franchise end dates:

[1] Awarded for six years to 2013 with an extension for a further two years and five months to 31 March 2016 if performance targets are met.

[2] Likely to be extended for four weeks to 28 April 2013 owing to engineering works at Reading over the Easter 2013 period.

[3] A new short-term Greater Anglia franchise commenced on 5 February 2012, operated by Abellio. This is due to run until July 2014 when a new 15-year franchise is due to start.

[4] Currently run on an interim basis by DfT management company Directly Operated Railways (trading as East Coast). This arrangement is due to continue until at least December 2013.

[5] The Virgin Trains franchise was due to end in December 2012 but the award of the new franchise to First Group was cancelled in October 2012 and at the time of writing it had not been decided whether Virgin Trains would should continue running the franchise or whether it should be taken over by the Government (Directly Operated Railways) on an interim basis.

[6] The London Rail Concession is different from other rail franchises, as fares and service levels are set by Transport for London instead of the DfT.

[7] Under the control of Merseytravel PTE instead of the DfT. Franchise reviewed every five years to fit in with the Merseyside Local Transport Plan.

[8] Franchise extended in 2011 to end between April 2014 and March 2015 to align with the end of the Trans-Pennine Express franchise.

[9] Upon termination of the Southern franchise in July 2015 it is to be combined with the Thameslink/Great Northern franchise.

[10] Awarded for seven years to 2014 with an extension for a further three years to 3 February 2017 if performance targets are met.

[11] Awarded for six years to 2012 with an extension for up to a further three years to 31 March 2015 if performance targets were met. This was cut by 18 months in 2011 so the franchise would finish in September 2013. The new franchise will be combined with Southern from July 2015.

[12] Originally awarded for eight years to 2012 with a possible extension for five years to 31 January 2017. The end date was revised in 2011 to be aligned with the end of the Northern franchise – the present contract will finish between April 2014 and March 2015.

[13] Awarded for six years to 2013 with an extension for a further two years to 19 September 2015 if performance targets are met.

All new franchises officially start at 02.00 on the first day, although the last dates shown above are the last full day of operation.

Where termination dates are dependent on performance targets being met, the earliest possible termination date is given. However, with Merseyrail the end date is based on the maximum franchise length.

The following operators run non-franchised services only:

Operator	Trading Name	Route
BAA	Heathrow Express	London Paddington–Heathrow Airport
First Hull Trains	First Hull Trains	London King's Cross–Hull
Grand Central	Grand Central	London King's Cross–Sunderland/ Bradford Interchange
North Yorkshire Moors Railway Enterprises	North Yorkshire Moors Railway	Pickering–Grosmont–Whitby/ Battersby
West Coast Railway Company	West Coast Railway Company	Birmingham–Stratford-upon-Avon* Fort William–Mallaig* York–Wakefield–York–Scarborough*

* Special summer services only.

INTERNATIONAL PASSENGER OPERATIONS

Eurostar (UK) operates passenger services between the UK and mainland Europe, jointly with the national operators of France (SNCF) and Belgium (SNCB/NMBS). Eurostar International is owned by three shareholders: SNCF (55%), London & Continental Railways (40%) and SNCB (5%).

In addition, a service for the conveyance of accompanied road vehicles through the Channel Tunnel is provided by the tunnel operating company, Eurotunnel.

FREIGHT TRAIN OPERATIONS

The following operators operate freight services or empty passenger stock workings under "Open Access" arrangements:

Colas Rail: In addition to its On-Track Machines and infrastructure activities, Colas Rail operates a number of freight flows, principally steel traffic to Boston using its Class 56s and coal from Wolsingham (on the Weardale Railway) to Scunthorpe and Ratcliffe plus timber from Carlisle, Ribblehead and Teignbridge to Chirk using its Class 56s or 66s. The small fleet of three Class 47s are used as required.

DB Schenker Rail (UK): Still the biggest freight operator in the country, DBS (formerly EWS before being bought by DB) has seen some of its core traffic lost to competitors in recent years. It is still the largest provider of infrastructure trains to Network Rail and operates coal, steel, intermodal and aggregate trains nationwide. The core fleet is Class 66s. Of the original 250 ordered around 180 are still used in the UK, with the remainder having moved to DB's French and Polish operations, although some of the French locos do return to the UK at times of high demand such as during the autumn. A small number of Class 60s are also used on the heavier trains, although more are currently being overhauled.

DBS's six Class 59/2s are used alongside the Mendip Rail 59/0s and 59/1s on stone traffic from the Mendip quarries and around the South-East. DBS's fleet of Class 67s are used on passenger or standby duties for Arriva Trains

Wales, Chiltern Railways, East Coast and ScotRail plus charter trains and a small number of freight duties. Class 90s are hired to ScotRail for use on the Sleeper services and also to Greater Anglia but see little use on freight, whilst the fleet of Class 92s are mainly used on intermodal duties, including a limited number of overnight trains on High Speed 1.

DBS also operates a number of both steam and diesel charter trains.

Devon & Cornwall Railway (a subsidiary of British American Railway Services): D&C operates scrap trains using its fleet of 56s and also provides locos from its fleet of 31s or 56s for empty stock moves.

Direct Rail Services: DRS has built on its original nuclear flask traffic to operate a number of different services. The main flows are intermodal (mostly Anglo-Scottish) plus the provision of crews and locos to Network Rail for autumn Railhead Treatment Trains. Its Class 47s are also used on charter work. DRS has the most varied fleet of locomotives of all the operators, with Class 20s, 37s, 47s, 57s and 66s. It also has 15 new Vossloh locomotives on order, to be designated Class 68.

Freightliner: Freightliner has two divisions: Intermodal operates container trains from the main Ports at Southampton, Felixstowe, Tilbury and Thamesport to major cities including London, Manchester, Leeds and Birmingham. The Heavy Haul division covers the movement of coal, cement, infrastructure and aggregates nationwide. Most services are worked by Class 66s, with new Class 70s used on some of the longer intermodal trains and some Heavy Haul flows, principally coal and cement. A small fleet of Class 86 and 90 electrics are used on intermodal trains on the Great Eastern and West Coast Main Lines, the Class 86s mainly being used in pairs on the WCML between Crewe and Coatbridge.

GB Railfreight: GBRf, formerly owned by First Group and now by Eurotunnel, operates a mixture of traffic types, mainly using Class 66s together with a small fleet of Class 73s used on infrastructure duties in the South-East. A growing fleet of Class 92s are also used on some intermodal flows to/from Dollands Moor. Traffic types include coal, intermodal, biomass and gypsum as well as infrastructure services for Network Rail and London Underground.

West Coast Railway Company: WCRC has a freight license but doesn't operate any freight as such – only empty stock movements. Its fleet of 47s, supplemented by a smaller number of 33s, 37s and 57s, are used on charter work nationwide, including the prestigious Royal Scotsman.

MAINTENANCE OF LOCOMOTIVES

Depot allocation codes for all locomotives are shown in this book (apart from shunters where the actual location of each is shown). It should be noted that today much locomotive maintenance is undertaken away from these depots. This may be undertaken at fuelling points, berthing sidings or similar, or by mobile maintenance teams. Therefore locomotives in particular may not return to their "home" depots (for example Toton for most DB Schenker locomotives) as often as in the past.

INTRODUCTION

SCOPE

This section contains details of all locomotives which can run on Britain's national railway network, plus those of Eurotunnel. Locomotives which are owned by, for example, DB Schenker and Freightliner which have been withdrawn from service and awaiting disposal are listed in the main part of the book. Locos which are awaiting disposal at scrapyards are listed in the "Locomotives Awaiting Disposal" section.

Only preserved locomotives which are currently used on the National Rail network are included. Others, which may still be Network Rail registered but not at present certified for use, are not included, but will be found in the Platform 5 book, "Preserved Locomotives and Multiple Units".

LOCOMOTIVE CLASSES

Locomotive classes are listed in numerical order of class. Principal details and dimensions are quoted for each class in metric and/or imperial units as considered appropriate bearing in mind common UK usage.

All dimensions and weights are quoted for locomotives in an "as new" condition with all necessary supplies (eg oil, water and sand) on board. Dimensions are quoted in the order length x width. Lengths quoted are over buffers or couplers as appropriate. All widths quoted are maxima. Where two different wheel diameter dimensions are shown, the first refers to powered wheels and the second refers to non-powered wheels.

NUMERICAL LISTINGS

Locomotives are listed in numerical order. Where numbers actually carried are different from those officially allocated, these are noted in class headings where appropriate. Where locomotives have been recently renumbered, the most immediate previous number is shown in parentheses. Each locomotive entry is laid out as in the following example:

RSL No.	Detail	Livery	Owner	Pool	Allocn.	Name
57304	d	**DS**	P	XHAC	KM	Pride of Cheshire

Detail Differences. Only detail differences which currently affect the areas and types of train which locomotives may work are shown. All other detail differences are excluded. Where such differences occur within a class or part class, they are shown in the "Detail" column alongside the individual locomotive number.

Standard abbreviations used for the locomotives section are:

a	Train air brake equipment only.
b	Drophead buckeye couplers.
c	Scharfenberg couplers.
d	Fitted with retractable Dellner couplers.
e	European Railway Traffic Management System (ERTMS) signalling equipment fitted.
k	Fitted with Swinghead Automatic "buckeye" combination couplers.
p	Train air, vacuum and electro-pneumatic brakes.
r	Radio Electric Token Block signalling equipment fitted.
s	Slow Speed Control equipment.
v	Train vacuum brake only.
x	Train air and vacuum brakes ("Dual brakes").
+	Additional fuel tank capacity.
§	Sandite laying equipment.

In all cases use of the above abbreviations indicates the equipment indicated is normally operable. Meaning of non-standard abbreviations and symbols is detailed in individual class headings.

Codes: Codes are used to denote the livery, owner, pool and depot of each locomotive. Details of these will be found in section 7 of this book. (S) denotes that the locomotive is currently stored.

Names: Only names carried with official sanction are listed. Names are shown in UPPER/lower case characters as actually shown on the name carried on the locomotive.

GENERAL INFORMATION

CLASSIFICATION AND NUMBERING

All locomotives are classified and allocated numbers by the Rolling Stock Library under the TOPS numbering system, introduced in 1972. This comprises a two-digit class number followed by a three-digit serial number. Where the actual number carried by a locomotive differs from the allocated number, or where an additional number is carried to the allocated number, this is shown by a note in the class heading.

For diesel locomotives, class numbers offer an indication of engine horsepower as shown in the table below.

Class No. Range	Engine hp
01–14	0–799
15–20	800–1000
21–31	1001–1499
32–39	1500–1999
40–54, 57	2000–2999
55–56, 58–70	3000+

For electric locomotives class numbers are allocated in ascending numerical order under the following scheme:

Class 71–80   Direct current and DC/diesel dual system locomotives.
Class 81 onwards   Alternating current and AC/DC dual system locos.

Numbers in the 89xxx series are allocated by the Rolling Stock Library to locomotives which have been de-registered but subsequently re-registered for use on the Network Rail network and whose original number has already been re-used. 89xxx numbers are normally only carried inside locomotive cabs and are not carried externally in normal circumstances.

WHEEL ARRANGEMENT

For main line locomotives the number of driven axles on a bogie or frame is denoted by a letter (A = 1, B = 2, C = 3 etc) and the number of non-powered axles is denoted by a number. The use of the letter "o" after a letter indicates each axle is individually powered, whilst the "+" symbol indicates bogies are inter-coupled.

For shunting locomotives, the Whyte notation is used. In this notation the number of leading wheels are given, followed by the number of driving wheels and then the trailing wheels.

HAULAGE CAPABILITY OF DIESEL LOCOMOTIVES

The haulage capability of a diesel locomotive depends upon three basic factors:

1. Adhesive weight. The greater the weight on the driving wheels, the greater the adhesion and more tractive power can be applied before wheelslip occurs.

2. The characteristics of its transmission. To start a train the locomotive has to exert a pull at standstill. A direct drive diesel engine cannot do this, hence the need for transmission. This may be mechanical, hydraulic or electric. The present British Standard for locomotives is electric transmission. Here the diesel engine drives a generator or alternator and the current produced is fed to the traction motors. The force produced by each driven wheel depends on the current in its traction motor. In other words, the larger the current, the harder it pulls. As the locomotive speed increases, the current in the traction motor falls, hence the *Maximum Tractive Effort* is the maximum force at its wheels the locomotive can exert at a standstill. The electrical equipment cannot take such high currents for long without overheating. Hence the *Continuous Tractive Effort* is quoted which represents the current which the equipment can take continuously.

3. The power of its engine. Not all power reaches the rail, as electrical machines are approximately 90% efficient. As the electrical energy passes through two such machines (the generator or alternator and the traction motors), the *Power at Rail* is approximately 81% (90% of 90%) of the engine power, less a further amount used for auxiliary equipment such as radiator fans, traction motor blowers, air compressors, battery charging, cab heating, Electric Train Supply (ETS) etc. The power of the locomotive is proportional to the tractive effort times the speed. Hence when on full power there is a speed corresponding to the continuous tractive effort.

HAULAGE CAPABILITY OF ELECTRIC LOCOMOTIVES

Unlike a diesel locomotive, an electric locomotive does not develop its power on board and its performance is determined only by two factors, namely its weight and the characteristics of its electrical equipment. Whereas a diesel locomotive tends to be a constant power machine, the power of an electric locomotive varies considerably. Up to a certain speed it can produce virtually a constant tractive effort. Hence power rises with speed according to the formula given in section three above, until a maximum speed is reached at which tractive effort falls, such that the power also falls. Hence the power at the speed corresponding to the maximum tractive effort is lower than the maximum speed.

BRAKE FORCE

The brake force is a measure of the braking power of a locomotive. This is shown on the locomotive data panels so operating staff can ensure sufficient brake power is available on freight trains.

ELECTRIC TRAIN SUPPLY (ETS)

A number of locomotives are equipped to provide a supply of electricity to the train being hauled to power auxiliaries such as heating, cooling fans, air conditioning and kitchen equipment. ETS is provided from the locomotive by means of a separate alternator (except Class 33 locos, which have a DC generator). The ETS index of a locomotive is a measure of the electrical power available for train supply.

Similarly, most loco-hauled coaches also have an ETS index, which in this case is a measure of the power required to operate equipment mounted in the coach. The sum of the ETS indices of all the hauled vehicles in a train must not exceed the ETS index of the locomotive.

ETS is commonly (but incorrectly) known as ETH (Electric Train Heating), which is a throwback to the days before loco-hauled coaches were equipped with electrically powered auxiliary equipment other than for train heating.

ROUTE AVAILABILITY (RA)

This is a measure of a railway vehicle's axle load. The higher the axle load of a vehicle, the higher the RA number on a scale from 1 to 10. Each Network Rail route has a RA number and in general no vehicle with a higher RA number may travel on that route without special clearance.

MULTIPLE & PUSH-PULL WORKING

Multiple working between vehicles (ie two or more powered vehicles being driven from one cab) is facilitated by jumper cables connecting the vehicles. However, not all types are compatible with each other, and a number of different systems are in use, each system being incompatible with any other.

Association of American Railroads (AAR) System: Classes 59, 66, 67 and 70.
Blue Star Coupling Code: Classes 20, 25, 31, 33, 37 40 and 73.
DRS System: Classes 20/3, 37, 47 and 57.
Green Circle Coupling Code: Class 47 (not all equipped).
Orange Square Coupling Code: Class 50.
Red Diamond Coupling Code: Classes 56 and 58.
SR System: Classes 33/1, 73 and various electric multiple units.
Within Own Class only: Classes 43 and 60.

Many locomotives use a time-division multiplex (TDM) system for push-pull and multiple working which utilises the existing RCH jumper cables fitted to coaching stock vehicles. Previously these cables had only been used to control train lighting and public address systems.

Class 47 locos 47701–47717 were equipped with an older non-standard TDM system.

1. DIESEL LOCOMOTIVES

CLASS 08   BR/ENGLISH ELECTRIC   0-6-0

Built: 1955–62 by BR at Crewe, Darlington, Derby Locomotive, Doncaster or Horwich Works.
Engine: English Electric 6KT of 298 kW (400 hp) at 680 rpm.
Main Generator: English Electric 801.
Traction Motors: Two English Electric 506.
Maximum Tractive Effort: 156 kN (35000 lbf).
Continuous Tractive Effort: 49 kN (11100 lbf) at 8.8 mph.
Power At Rail: 194 kW (260 hp).   **Train Brakes:** Air & vacuum.
Brake Force: 19 t.   **Dimensions:** 8.92 x 2.59 m.
Weight: 49.6–50.4 t.   **Wheel Diameter:** 1372 mm.
Design Speed: 20 mph.   **Maximum Speed:** 15 mph.
Fuel Capacity: 3037 litres.   **RA:** 5.
Train Supply: Not equipped.
Multiple Working: m Equipped for multiple working. All others not equipped.

Notes: † – Fitted with remote control equipment.

For shunting locomotives, instead of the two-letter depot code, actual locations at the time of publication are given.

Class 08s that don't have current Network Rail engineering acceptance are considered to be "in industrial service" and can be found in section 4 of this book.

08850 has acceptance for use between Battersby and Whitby only, for rescue purposes.

Non-standard liveries/numbering:

08308	All over ScotRail "Caledonian Sleeper" purple.
08480	Yellow with a red bodyside band. Carries number "TOTON No 1".
08616	Carries number 3783.
08696	Carries no number.
08701	Carries number "Tyne 100".
08721	As **B**, but with a black roof & "Express parcels" branding with red & yellow stripe.
08824	Carries number "IEMD01".

Originally numbered in series D3000–D4192.

Class 08/0. Standard Design.

08077	**FL**	P	DHLT	LH Group, Barton-under-Needwood (S)
08308 a	**0**	RL	MRSO	Inverness Depot
08405 a†	**E**	DB	WSSK	Carlisle Yards
08410 a	**FB**	FW	EFSH	Penzance Long Rock Depot
08428 a	**E**	DB	WSSK	Doncaster Yards
08451	**B**	AM	ATLO	Manchester Longsight Depot
08454	**K**	AM	ATLO	Manchester Longsight Depot

▲ EWS-liveried 08752, one of the DB Schenker Class 08s fitted with remote control equipment, stands in Didcot Yard on 25/07/12. **Stewart Armstrong**

▼ 08950, one of four East Midlands Trains 08s based at Neville Hill, shunts the prototype HST power car 41000 within the depot on 29/03/12. **Tony Shaw**

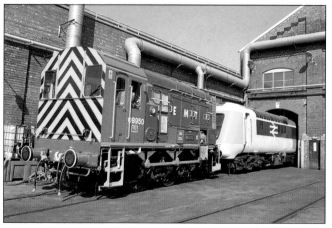

▲ Owned by GBRf, BR Green liveried 09002/009 are based at Trafford Park. On 07/12/11 09009 draws out of the Barton Dock terminal with a container train for Felixstowe that will be taken forward by 66741. **Hugh Ballantyne**

▼ Network Rail yellow-liveried 31465 and 31106 in BR Blue top-and-tail a Derby–Derby via Corby and Bletchley test train at Barrow-upon-Soar on 07/08/12. **Joshua Day**

▲ Harry Needle Railroad Company 20311/314 and 20096/107 top-and-tail two tanks used as barriers for LUL stock moves near Wellingborough on 03/10/12, working from West Ruislip to Derby. The two leading 20s are in HNRC livery and those on the rear are in BR Blue.

Nigel Gibbs

▲ West Coast Railway Company-liveried 37706 passes Kinloid working the Spean Bridge–Mallaig leg of the Royal Scotsman luxury train on 26/05/12.

Neil Gibson

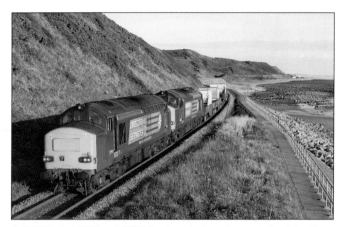

▲ DRS-liveried 37611 and 37612 head north along the scenic Cumbrian Coast near St Bees with 6C46 19.36 Sellafield–Carlisle Kingmoor train of nuclear flasks on 14/08/12. **Eliot Anderson**

▼ 43013 and 43062 work the Network Rail New Measurement Train south on the West Coast Main Line at Oubeck on 15/08/12. The train was running from Glasgow Central to Crewe. **Fred Kerr**

▲ East Midlands Trains-liveried HST 43043/055 pass Moorhouse, near South Elmsall, with the 13.50 (Sun) Leeds–London St Pancras on 01/05/11. **Robert Pritchard**

▲ WCRC Maroon 47854 "Diamond Jubilee" passes Abington whilst working a Fort William–Bristol railtour on 07/10/12. **Stuart Fowler**

▼ Two DRS Class 47s carry Northern Belle livery. On 08/09/12 47832 "Solway Princess" leads a Gobowen–Bath Spa excursion on the approach to Banbury. **Nigel Gibbs**

▲ BR Blue-liveried 50044 "Exeter" heads a Paignton–Cardiff GBRf charter at Newton Abbot West Junction on 21/07/12 as a FGW HST (43155/190) is alongside working the 15.52 Penzance–London Paddington.   **David Hunt**

▼ First Great Western 57602 "Restormel Castle" is seen on the rear of the FGW Sleeper as the stock is hauled out of Paddington to Old Oak Common depot on 26/05/12.   **Mark Beal**

08472 a	**WA**	WA	RFSH	Edinburgh Craigentinny Depot
08480 a	**0**	DB	WNYX	Toton Depot (S)
08483 a	**GL**	FW	EFSH	Old Oak Common HST Depot
08495 †	**E**	DB	WSSK	Eastleigh Yards
08500	**E**	DB	WNYX	Tees Yard (S)
08525	**ST**	EM	EMSL	Leeds Neville Hill Depot
08530	**FL**	P	DFLS	Tilbury FLT
08531 a	**FL**	P	DFLS	LH Group, Barton-under-Needwood
08567	**E**	DB	WSSK	Mossend Yard
08571 a	**WA**	WA	HBSH	Bounds Green Depot
08575	**FL**	P	DHLT	Southampton Maritime FLT (S)
08578 †	**E**	DB	WNXX	Toton Depot (S)
08580	**E**	DB	WNXX	Bescot Depot (S)
08585	**FL**	P	DFLS	LH Group, Barton-under-Needwood
08593	**E**	DB	WNXX	Crewe International Depot (S)
08596 a†	**WA**	WA	RFSH	Bounds Green Depot
08605	**E**	DB	WSSK	Toton Yards
08611	**V**	AM	ATLO	Manchester Longsight Depot
08615	**WA**	WA	RFSH	Edinburgh Craigentinny Depot
08616	**LM**	LM	EJLO	Birmingham Tyseley Depot
08617	**K**	AM	ATLO	Wembley Depot
08623	**E**	DB	WNYX	Crewe International Depot (S)
08624	**FL**	P	DFLS	Trafford Park FLT
08630	**E**	DB	WNXX	Toton Yards (S)
08632 †	**E**	DB	WSSK	Mountsorrel Stone Terminal
08633 †	**E**	DB	WSSK	Westbury Yards
08641	**FB**	FW	EFSH	Plymouth Laira Depot
08644	**GL**	FW	EFSH	Plymouth Laira Depot
08645	**FB**	FW	EFSH	Plymouth Laira Depot
08653	**E**	DB	WNXX	Toton Yards (S)
08663 a	**FB**	FW	EFSH	Bristol St Philip's Marsh Depot
08669 a	**WA**	WA	RFSH	Wabtec Rail, Doncaster Works
08676	**E**	DB	WSSL	Mossend Yard
08690	**ST**	EM	EMSL	Leeds Neville Hill Depot
08691	**FL**	FL	DFLS	Felixstowe FLT
08696 a	**G**	AM	ATLO	Wembley Depot
08701 a	**RX**	DB	WNXX	Toton Yards (S)
08703 a	**E**	DB	WSSK	Hoo Junction Yards
08706 †	**E**	DB	WNYX	Crewe International Depot (S)
08709	**E**	DB	WNXX	Bescot Depot (S)
08711 k	**RX**	DB	WNXX	Tees Yard (S)
08714	**E**	DB	WSXX	Axiom Rail, Stoke-on-Trent Works (S)
08721	**0**	AM	ATLO	Liverpool Edge Hill Depot
08724	**WA**	WA	HBSH	Leeds Neville Hill Depot
08735 †	**E**	DB	WNYX	Eastleigh Yards (S)
08737 a	**E**	DB	WSSI	Margam Yard
08738 m	**ECR**	DB	WNTS	Toton Yards (S)
08742 †	**RX**	DB	WNYX	Crewe International Depot (S)
08752 †	**E**	DB	WSSK	Didcot Yards
08757	**RG**	DB	WNYX	Didcot Yards (S)
08782 a†	**CU**	DB	WSSI	Scunthorpe Yard

08784 †	E	DB	WNTS	Toton Depot (S)
08785 a	FL	P	DFLS	Southampton Maritime FLT
08788	K	RL	MRSO	Inverness Depot
08790	B	AM	ATLO	Wolverhampton Oxley Depot
08795	GL	FW	EFSH	Swansea Landore Depot
08799 a	E	DB	WNYX	Toton Yards (S)
08802 †	E	DB	WSSL	Dagenham Yards
08804 †	E	DB	WSSK	Doncaster Yards
08805	B	LM	EJLO	Birmingham Soho Depot
08822	FB	FW	EFSH	Bristol St Philip's Marsh Depot
08824 ak	K	DB	WSXX	Crewe International Depot (S)
08836	FB	FW	EFSH	Old Oak Common HST Depot
08847	CD	RL	MRSO	Norwich Crown Point Depot
08850	B	NY	MBDL	Grosmont Depot
08853 a	WA	WA	RFSH	Wabtec Rail, Doncaster Works
08865	E	DB	WSSK	Bescot Yards
08873	RX	HU	DFLS	Southampton Maritime FLT
08874	SL	RL	MRSO	Norwich Crown Point Depot
08877	DG	DB	WSXX	Wigan Springs Branch Depot (S)
08879	E	DB	WSSK	Warrington Yards
08886 †	E	DB	WNXX	Crewe International Depot (S)
08887 a	VP	AM	ATZZ	Wembley Depot (S)
08888 †	E	DB	WSSI	Immingham Depot
08891	FL	P	DHLT	LH Group, Barton-under-Needwood (S)
08899	MA	EM	EMSL	Derby Etches Park Depot
08904	E	DB	WNYX	Crewe International Depot (S)
08907	E	DB	WSSL	Fowey Docks
08908	ST	EM	EMSL	Leeds Neville Hill Depot
08922	DG	DB	WNTS	Toton Depot (S)
08925	B	GB	GBWM	St Leonards Depot
08934 a	VP	GB	GBWM	Cardiff Tidal Steelworks
08939 m	ECR	DB	WNTS	Toton Yards (S)
08948 c	EP	EU	GPSS	Temple Mills Depot
08950	ST	EM	EMSL	Leeds Neville Hill Depot

Class 08/9. Reduced height cab. Converted 1985–87 by BR at Landore.

08993	E	DB	WNTS	Doncaster Depot (S)
08994 a	E	DB	WNTS	Toton Depot (S)
08995 a	E	DB	WSSK	Hoo Junction Yards

CLASS 09   BR/ENGLISH ELECTRIC   0-6-0

Built: 1959–62 by BR at Darlington or Horwich Works.
Engine: English Electric 6KT of 298 kW (400 hp) at 680 rpm.
Main Generator: English Electric 801.
Traction Motors: English Electric 506.
Maximum Tractive Effort: 111 kN (25000 lbf).
Continuous Tractive Effort: 39 kN (8800 lbf) at 11.6 mph.
Power At Rail: 201 kW (269 hp).   **Train Brakes:** Air & vacuum.
Brake Force: 19 t.   **Dimensions:** 8.92 x 2.59 m.
Weight: 49 t.   **Wheel Diameter:** 1372 mm.
Design Speed: 27 mph.   **Maximum Speed:** 27 mph.
Fuel Capacity: 3037 litres.   **RA:** 5.
Train Supply: Not equipped.   **Multiple Working:** Not equipped.

Notes: Class 09s that don't have current Network Rail engineering acceptance
are considered to be "in industrial service" and can be found in section 4 of
this book.

Class 09/0 were originally numbered D3665–D3671, D3719–D3721, D4099–
D4114.

Class 09/0. Built as Class 09.

09002	G	GB	GBWM	Trafford Park (Barton Dock) FLT
09006	E	DB	WNXX	Doncaster Depot (S)
09009	G	GB	GBWM	Trafford Park (Barton Dock) FLT
09026 a	G	SN	HWSU	Brighton Lovers Walk Depot

Class 09/1. Converted from Class 08. 110 V electrical equipment.
Converted: 1992–1993 by RFS Industries, Kilnhurst.

09106 (08759)	E	DB	WSSL	Hams Hall Distribution Park, Coleshill

Class 09/2. Converted from Class 08. 90 V electrical equipment.
Converted: 1992 by RFS Industries, Kilnhurst.

09201 (08421) ak	DG	DB	WSSI	Knottingley Depot

Class 08 and Class 09 names:

08451	M.A. SMITH	08691	Terri
08483	DUSTY Driver David Miller	08721	DOWNHILL C.S.
08495	NOEL KIRTON OBE	08782	CASTLETON WORKS
08525	DUNCAN BEDFORD	08790	Steve Purser
08585	Vicky	08799	FRED
08616	TYSELEY 100	08805	CONCORDE
08630	BOB BROWN	08874	Catherine
08645	Mike Baggott	08908	IVAN STEPHENSON
08669	Bob Machin	08950	DAVID LIGHTFOOT
08690	DAVID THIRKILL	09026	Cedric Wares

CLASS 20   ENGLISH ELECTRIC   Bo-Bo

Built: 1957–68 by English Electric at Vulcan Foundry, Newton-le-Willows or by Robert Stephenson & Hawthorns at Darlington.
Engine: English Electric 8SVT Mk II of 746 kW (1000 hp) at 850 rpm.
Main Generator: English Electric 819/3C.
Traction Motors: English Electric 526/5D or 526/8D.
Maximum Tractive Effort: 187 kN (42000 lbf).
Continuous Tractive Effort: 111 kN (25000 lbf) at 11 mph.
Power At Rail: 574 kW (770 hp).   **Train Brakes:** Air & vacuum.
Brake Force: 35 t.   **Dimensions:** 14.25 x 2.67 m.
Weight: 73.4–73.5 t.   **Wheel Diameter:** 1092 mm.
Design Speed: 75 mph.   **Maximum Speed:** 75 mph.
Fuel Capacity: 1727 litres.   **RA:** 5.
Train Supply: Not equipped.   **Multiple Working:** Blue Star.

Originally numbered in series D8007–D8190, D8315–D8325.

Non-standard livery/numbering:

20088 RFS grey (carries No. 2017).
20906 Carries no number.

Class 20/0. Standard Design.

20016	B	HN	HNRS	LM (S)
20057	B	HN	HNRS	LM (S)
20081	B	HN	HNRS	LM (S)
20088	0	HN	HNRS	LM (S)
20092	U	HN	HNRS	LM (S)
20096	B	HN	GBEE	BH
20107	B	HN	GBEE	BH
20118	F0	HN	HNRL	BH	Saltburn-by-the-Sea
20132	F0	HN	HNRL	BH	
20142	B	20	GBEE	SK
20189	G	20	GBEE	SK
20227	F0	2L	GBEE	SK

Class 20/3. Direct Rail Services refurbished locos. Details as Class 20/0 except:

Refurbished: 1995–96 by Brush Traction at Loughborough (20301–305) or 1997–98 by RFS(E) at Doncaster (20306–315). Disc indicators or headcode panels removed.
Train Brakes: Air.   **Maximum Speed:** 60 mph (+ 75 mph).
Weight: 73 t (+ 76 t).   **Fuel Capacity:** 2909 (+ 4909) litres.
Brake Force: 35 t (+ 31 t).   **RA:** 5 (+ 6).
Multiple Working: DRS system.

20301	(20047)	r	**DS**	DR	XHNC	KM	Max Joule 1958–1999
20302	(20084)	r	**DS**	DR	XHNC	KM	
20303	(20127)	r	**DR**	DR	XHNC	KM	
20304	(20120)	r	**DR**	DR	XHNC	KM	
20305	(20095)	r	**DS**	DR	XHNC	KM	Gresty Bridge
20306	(20131)	r+	**DR**	DR	XHSS	BH (S)	

20307	(20128) r+	**DR**	DR	XHSS	KM (S)
20308	(20187) r+	**DS**	DR	XHNC	KM
20309	(20075) r+	**DS**	DR	XHSS	KM (S)
20310	(20190) r+	**DR**	DR	XHSS	KM (S)
20311	(20102) r+	**HN**	HN	GBEE	BH
20312	(20042) r+	**DS**	DR	XHNC	KM
20313	(20194) r+	**DR**	DR	XHSS	KM (S)
20314	(20117) r+	**HN**	HN	GBEE	BH
20315	(20104) r+	**DR**	DR	XHSS	KM (S)

Class 20/9. Harry Needle Railroad Company (former Hunslet-Barclay/ DRS) locos. Details as Class 20/0 except:

Refurbished: 1989 by Hunslet-Barclay at Kilmarnock.
Train Brakes: Air.   **Fuel Capacity:** 1727 (+ 4727) litres.
RA: 5 (+ 6).

20901	(20101)	**GB**	HN	GBEE	BH
20903	(20083) +	**DR**	HN	HNRS	BO (S)
20904	(20041)	**DR**	HN	HNRS	BO (S)
20905	(20225) +	**GB**	HN	GBEE	BH
20906	(20219)	**DR**	HN	HNRS	BH (S)

CLASS 25   BR/BEYER PEACOCK/SULZER   Bo-Bo

Built: 1965 by Beyer Peacock at Gorton.
Engine: Sulzer 6LDA28-B of 930 kW (1250 hp) at 750 rpm.
Main Generator: AEI RTB15656.   **Traction Motors:** AEI 253AY.
Maximum Tractive Effort: 200 kN (45000 lbf).
Continuous Tractive Effort: 93 kN (20800 lbf) at 17.1 mph.
Power At Rail: 708 kW (949 hp).   **Train Brakes:** Air & vacuum.
Brake Force: 38 t.   **Dimensions:** 15.39 x 2.73 m.
Weight: 71.5 t.   **Wheel Diameter:** 1143 mm.
Design Speed: 90 mph.   **Maximum Speed:** 60 mph.
Fuel Capacity: 2270 litres.   **RA:** 5.
Train Supply: Not equipped.   **Multiple Working:** Blue Star.

Original number is D7628, which the loco currently carries.

Note: Only certified for use on Network Rail metals between Whitby and Battersby, as an extension of North Yorkshire Moors Railway services.

25278	**GG**	NY	MBDL	NY	SYBILLA

CLASS 31   BRUSH/ENGLISH ELECTRIC   A1A-A1A

Built: 1958–62 by Brush Traction at Loughborough.
Engine: English Electric 12SVT of 1100 kW (1470 hp) at 850 rpm.
Main Generator: Brush TG160-48.   **Traction Motors:** Brush TM73-68.
Maximum Tractive Effort: 160 kN (35900 lbf).
Continuous Tractive Effort: 83 kN (18700 lbf) at 23.5 mph.
Power At Rail: 872 kW (1170 hp).   **Train Brakes:** Air & vacuum.

Brake Force: 49 t.
Weight: 106.7–111 t.
Design Speed: 90 mph.
Fuel Capacity: 2409 litres.
Train Supply: Not equipped.

Dimensions: 17.30 x 2.67 m.
Wheel Diameter: 1092/1003 mm.
Maximum Speed: 90 mph.
RA: 5 or 6.
Multiple Working: Blue Star.

Originally numbered D5520–D5699, D5800–D5862 (not in order).

Non-standard numbering:

31190 Also carries number D5613.

Class 31/1. Standard Design. RA: 5.

31105	Y	NR	QADD	ZA	
31106 a	B	RE	RVLO	ZA	
31128	B	NS	NRLO	NY	CHARYBDIS
31190	G	BA	HTLX	WH	
31233 a	Y	NR	QADD	ZA	
31285	Y	NR	QADD	ZA	

Class 31/4. Electric Train Supply equipment. RA: 6.
Train Supply: Electric, index 66.

31422	IC	RE	RVLO	ZA (S)	
31452	DC	BA	RVLO	ZA	
31454	IC	BA	HTLX	WH	
31459	K	RE	RVLO	ZA	CERBERUS
31465	Y	NR	QADD	ZA	
31468	FR	BA	RVLO	WO (S)	HYDRA

Class 31/6. ETS through wiring and controls. RA: 5.

31601 (31186)	DC	BA	HTLX	WH	
31602 (31191)	Y	RE	RVLO	ZA	

CLASS 33   BRCW/SULZER   Bo-Bo

Built: 1960–62 by the Birmingham Railway Carriage & Wagon Company at Smethwick.
Engine: Sulzer 8LDA28 of 1160 kW (1550 hp) at 750 rpm.
Main Generator: Crompton Parkinson CG391B1.
Traction Motors: Crompton Parkinson C171C2.
Maximum Tractive Effort: 200 kN (45000 lbf).
Continuous Tractive Effort: 116 kN (26000 lbf) at 17.5 mph.
Power At Rail: 906 kW (1215 hp).
Brake Force: 35 t.
Weight: 76-78 t.
Design Speed: 85 mph.
Fuel Capacity: 3410 litres.
Train Supply: Electric, index 48 (750 V DC only).
Multiple Working: Blue Star.

Train Brakes: Air & vacuum.
Dimensions: 15.47 x 2.82 (2.64 m 33/2).
Wheel Diameter: 1092 mm.
Maximum Speed: 85 mph.
RA: 6.

Originally numbered in series D6500–D6597 but not in order.

Non-standard numbering:

33012 Carries number D6515.

Class 33/0. Standard Design.

33012	**G**	71	MBDL	Swanage Rly	
33025	**WC**	WC	MBDL	CS	Glen Falloch
33029	**WC**	WC	MBDL	CS	Glen Loy
33030	**DR**	WC	MBDL	CS (S)	

Class 33/2. Built to former Loading Gauge of Tonbridge–Battle Line.
Equipped with slow speed control.

33207	**WC**	WC	MBDL	CS	Jim Martin

CLASS 37   ENGLISH ELECTRIC   Co-Co

Built: 1960–66 by English Electric at Vulcan Foundry, Newton-le-Willows or by Robert Stephenson & Hawthorns at Darlington.
Engine: English Electric 12CSVT of 1300 kW (1750 hp) at 850 rpm.
Main Generator: English Electric 822/10G.
Traction Motors: English Electric 538/A.
Maximum Tractive Effort: 245 kN (55500 lbf).
Continuous Tractive Effort: 156 kN (35000 lbf) at 13.6 mph.
Power At Rail: 932 kW (1250 hp).   **Train Brakes:** Air & vacuum.
Brake Force: 50 t.   **Dimensions:** 18.75 x 2.74 m.
Weight: 102.8–108.4 t.   **Wheel Diameter:** 1092 mm.
Design Speed: 90 mph.   **Maximum Speed:** 80 mph.
Fuel Capacity: 4046 (+ 7683) litres.   **RA:** 5 (§ 6).
Train Supply: Not equipped.
Multiple Working: Blue Star († DRS system).

Originally numbered D6600–D6608, D6700–D6999 (not in order).

Non-standard liveries/numbering:

37402 Light grey lower bodyside & dark grey upper bodyside.
37411 Also carries number D6990.

Class 37/0. Standard Design. Details as above.

37038	a†	**DR**	DR	XHNC	KM	
37059	ar+†**DS**		DR	XHSS	BH (S)	
37069	ar+†**DS**		DR	XHSS	CR (S)	
37087	a+	**DR**	DR	XHSS	BH (S)	Keighley & Worth Valley Railway 40th Anniversary 1968–2008
37165	a+	**CE**	WC	MBDL	CS (S)	
37194	a+	**DS**	DR	XHNC	KM	
37198	+	**Y**	NR	MBDL	GCR	
37214		**WC**	WC	MBDL	CS (S)	Loch Laidon
37218	ar+†**DS**		DR	XHNC	KM	
37229	a+	**DS**	DR	XHNC	KM	Jonty Jarvis 8-12-1998 to 18-3-2005
37259	ar†	**DS**	DR	XHNC	KM	
37261	a+	**DS**	DR	XHSS	KM (S)	

Class 37/4. Refurbished with electric train supply equipment. Main generator replaced by alternator. Regeared (CP7) bogies. Details as Class 37/0 except:
Main Alternator: Brush BA1005A.   **Power At Rail:** 935 kW (1254 hp).
Traction Motors: English Electric 538/5A.
Maximum Tractive Effort: 256 kN (57440 lbf).
Continuous Tractive Effort: 184 kN (41250 lbf) at 11.4 mph.
Weight: 107 t.   **Design Speed:** 80 mph.
Fuel Capacity: 7683 litres.
Train Supply: Electric, index 30.

37401	ar	**E**	DR	XHHP	KM (S)
37402	a	**0**	DR	XHHP	BH (S)
37405	ar	**E**	DR	XHHP	BH (S)
37406	ar	**E**	DR	XHHP	KM (S)
37409	ar†	**DS**	DR	XHAC	KM	Lord Hinton
37410	ar	**E**	DR	XHHP	KM (S)
37411	ar	**G**	DR	XHHP	KM (S)
37415		**E**	HN	HNRS	LM (S)
37416	ar	**GS**	DR	XHHP	KM (S)
37417	ar	**E**	DR	XHHP	KM (S)
37419	ar	**DS**	DR	XHAC	KM	Carl Haviland 1954–2012
37422	ar	**E**	DR	XHHP	KM (S)
37423	ar†	**DS**	DR	XHAC	KM	Spirit of the Lakes
37425	ar	**DS**	DR	XHAC	KM
37426	a	**E**	DR	XHHP	KM (S)
37427	ar	**E**	DR	XHHP	KM (S)
37428		**GS**	HN	HNRS	LM (S)

Class 37/5. Refurbished without train supply equipment. Main generator replaced by alternator. Regeared (CP7) bogies. Details as Class 37/4 except:
Maximum Tractive Effort: 248 kN (55590 lbf).
Weight: 106.1–110.0 t.

37503	r§	**E**	HN	HNRS	BH (S)
37510	a	**DS**	DR	XHSS	BH (S)
37516	s	**WC**	WC	MBDL	CS
37517	as	**LH**	WC	MBDL	CS (S)
37518	ar	**IC**	IR	MBDL	BQ	Fort William/An Gearasdan
37521	r§	**E**	HN	HNRS	BH (S)

Class 37/6. Originally refurbished for Nightstar services. Main generator replaced by alternator. UIC jumpers. Details as Class 37/5 except:
Maximum Speed: 90 mph.   **Train Brake:** Air.
Train Supply: Not equipped, but electric through wired.
Multiple Working: DRS system.

37601	a	**DS**	DR	XHNC	KM	Class 37-'Fifty'
37602	ar	**DS**	DR	XHNC	KM
37603	a	**DS**	DR	XHNC	KM
37604	a	**DS**	DR	XHNC	KM
37605	ar	**DS**	DR	XHNC	KM
37606	a	**DS**	DR	XHNC	KM
37607	ar	**DS**	DR	XHNC	KM

37608 ar	**DS**	DR	XHNC	KM	
37609 a	**DS**	DR	XHNC	KM	
37610 ar	**DS**	DR	XHNC	KM	T.S.(Ted) Cassady 14.5.61–6.4.08
37611 a	**DS**	DR	XHNC	KM	
37612 a	**DS**	DR	XHNC	KM	

Class 37/5 continued.

37667 ast	**DS**	DR	XHNC	KM	
37668 s	**E**	WC	MBDL	CS (S)	
37669 r	**E**	WC	MBDL	CS (S)	
37670 r	**DB**	HN	HNRS	EMR, Kingsbury (S)	
37676 r	**WC**	WC	MBDL	CS	Loch Rannoch
37682 ar	**DS**	DR	XHNC	KM	
37683 a	**DS**	DR	XHHP	ZA (S)	
37685 a	**WC**	WC	MBDL	CS	Loch Arkaig
37688 art	**DS**	DR	XHNC	KM	Kingmoor TMD
37696 as	**F**	HN	HNRS	LM (S)	

Class 37/7. Refurbished locos. Main generator replaced by alternator. Regeared (CP7) bogies. Ballast weights added. Details as Class 37/5 except:
Main Alternator: GEC G564AZ (37796–803) Brush BA1005A (others).
Maximum Tractive Effort: 276 kN (62000 lbf).
Weight: 120 t.   **RA:** 7.

37703	**GIF**	DB	WZKS	DL (S)	
37706	**WC**	WC	MBDL	CS	
37710	**LH**	WC	MBDL	CS (S)	
37712 a	**WC**	WC	MBDL	CS (S)	
37714	**GIF**	DB	WZKS	DL (S)	
37716	**GIF**	DB	WZKS	DL (S)	
37718	**GIF**	DB	WZKS	DL (S)	
37800	**GIF**	DB	WZKS	DL (S)	
37884	**GIF**	DB	WZKS	DL (S)	

Class 97/3. Class 37s refurbished for Network Rail for use on the Cambrian Lines pilot ERTMS signalling project. Details as Class 37/0.

97301 (37100)		**Y**	NR	QETS	ZA	
97302 (37170) e		**Y**	NR	QETS	ZA	
97303 (37178) e		**Y**	NR	QETS	ZA	
97304 (37217) e		**Y**	NR	QETS	ZA	John Tiley

CLASS 40   ENGLISH ELECTRIC   1Co-Co1

Built: 1958–62 by English Electric at Vulcan Foundry, Newton-le-Willows.
Engine: English Electric 16SVT Mk2 of 1490 kW (2000 hp) at 850 rpm.
Main Generator: English Electric 822/4C.
Traction Motors: English Electric 526/5D or EE526/7D.
Maximum Tractive Effort: 231 kN (52000 lbf).
Continuous Tractive Effort: 137 kN (30900 lbf) at 18.8 mph.
Power At Rail: 1160 kW (1550 hp).   **Train Brakes:** Air & vacuum.
Brake Force: 51 t.   **Dimensions:** 21.18 x 2.78 m.
Weight: 132 t.   **Wheel Diameter:** 914/1143 mm.
Design Speed: 90 mph.   **Maximum Speed:** 90 mph.
Fuel Capacity: 3250 litres.   **RA:** 6.
Train Supply: Steam.   **Multiple Working:** Blue Star.

Originally numbered D345.

40145	**BL**	40	ELRD	BQ	East Lancashire Railway

CLASS 43   BREL/PAXMAN   Bo-Bo

Built: 1975–82 by BREL at Crewe Works.
Engine: MTU 16V4000R41R of 1680kW (2250 hp) at 1500 rpm.
(* Paxman 12VP185 of 1565 kW (2100 hp) at 1500 rpm.)
Main Alternator: Brush BA1001B.
Traction Motors: Brush TMH68–46 or GEC G417AZ, frame mounted.
Maximum Tractive Effort: 80 kN (17980 lbf)
Continuous Tractive Effort: 46 kN (10340 lbf) at 64.5 mph.
Power At Rail: 1320 kW (1770 hp).   **Train Brakes:** Air.
Brake Force: 35 t.   **Dimensions:** 17.79 x 2.74 m.
Weight: 70.25 t.   **Wheel Diameter:** 1020 mm.
Design Speed: 125 mph.   **Maximum Speed:** 125 mph.
Fuel Capacity: 4500 litres.   **RA:** 5.
Train Supply: Three-phase electric.
Multiple Working: Within class, jumpers at non-driving end only.

Notes: † Buffer fitted.

43013, 43014 & 43062 are fitted with measuring apparatus & front-end cameras.

43002	**FB**	A	EFPC	LA	
43003	**FB**	A	EFPC	LA	ISAMBARD KINGDOM BRUNEL
43004	**FB**	A	EFPC	LA	First for the future/
					First ar gyfer y dyfodol
43005	**FB**	A	EFPC	LA	
43009	**FB**	A	EFPC	LA	First transforming travel
43010	**FB**	A	EFPC	LA	
43012	**FB**	A	EFPC	LA	
43013 †	**Y**	P	QCAR	EC	
43014 †	**Y**	P	QCAR	EC	
43015	**FB**	A	EFPC	LA	
43016	**FB**	A	EFPC	LA	
43017	**FB**	A	EFPC	LA	

43018		**FB**	A	EFPC	LA	
43020		**FB**	A	EFPC	LA	MTU Power. Passion. Partnership
43021		**FB**	A	EFPC	LA	David Austin – Cartoonist
43022		**FB**	A	EFPC	LA	
43023		**FB**	A	EFPC	LA	
43024		**FB**	A	EFPC	LA	Great Western Society 1961–2011
						Didcot Railway Centre
43025		**FB**	A	EFPC	LA	IRO The Institution of Railway Operators
						2000–2010 TEN YEARS
						PROMOTING OPERATIONAL EXCELLENCE
43026		**FB**	A	EFPC	LA	
43027		**FB**	A	EFPC	LA	Glorious Devon
43028		**FB**	A	EFPC	LA	
43029		**FB**	A	EFPC	LA	
43030		**FB**	A	EFPC	LA	Christian Lewis Trust
43031		**FB**	A	EFPC	LA	
43032		**FB**	A	EFPC	LA	
43033		**FB**	A	EFPC	LA	Driver Brian Cooper
						15 June 1947–5 October 1999
43034		**FB**	A	EFPC	LA	TravelWatch SouthWest
43035		**FB**	A	EFPC	LA	
43036		**FB**	A	EFPC	LA	
43037		**FB**	A	EFPC	LA	PENYDARREN
43040		**FB**	A	EFPC	LA	Bristol St. Philip's Marsh
43041		**FB**	A	EFPC	OO	Meningitis Trust Support for Life
43042		**FB**	A	EFPC	OO	
43043	*	**ST**	P	EMPC	NL	
43044	*	**ST**	P	EMPC	NL	
43045	*	**ST**	P	EMPC	NL	
43046	*	**ST**	P	EMPC	NL	
43047	*	**ST**	P	EMPC	NL	
43048	*	**ST**	P	EMPC	NL	T.C.B. Miller MBE
43049	*	**ST**	P	EMPC	NL	Neville Hill
43050	*	**ST**	P	EMPC	NL	
43052	*	**ST**	P	EMPC	NL	
43053		**FB**	P	EFPC	LE	University of Worcester
43054	*	**ST**	P	EMPC	NL	
43055	*	**ST**	P	EMPC	NL	The Sheffield Star 125 Years
43056		**FB**	P	EFPC	LE	The Royal British Legion
43058	*	**ST**	P	EMPC	NL	
43059	*	**ST**	P	EMPC	NL	
43060	*	**ST**	P	EMPC	NL	
43061	*	**ST**	P	EMPC	NL	
43062		**Y**	P	QCAR	EC	John Armitt
43063		**FB**	P	EFPC	OO	
43064	*	**ST**	P	EMPC	NL	
43066	*	**ST**	P	EMPC	NL	
43069		**FB**	P	EFPC	OO	
43070		**FB**	P	EFPC	OO	The Corps of Royal Electrical and
						Mechanical Engineers

43071		**FB**	P	EFPC	OO	
43073	*	**ST**	P	EMPC	NL	
43075	*	**ST**	P	EMPC	NL	
43076	*	**ST**	P	EMPC	NL	IN SUPPORT OF HELP for HEROES
43078		**FB**	P	EFPC	OO	
43079		**FB**	P	EFPC	OO	
43081	*	**ST**	P	EMPC	NL	
43082	*	**ST**	P	EMPC	NL	RAILWAY children – THE VOICE FOR STREET CHILDREN WORLDWIDE
43083	*	**ST**	P	EMPC	NL	
43086		**FB**	P	EFPC	OO	
43087		**FB**	P	EFPC	OO	11 Explosive Ordnance Disposal Regiment Royal Logistic Corps
43088		**FB**	P	EFPC	OO	
43089	*	**ST**	P	EMPC	NL	
43091		**FB**	P	EFPC	OO	
43092		**FB**	FG	EFPC	OO	
43093		**FB**	FG	EFPC	OO	
43094		**FB**	FG	EFPC	OO	
43097		**FB**	FG	EFPC	OO	Environment Agency
43098		**FB**	FG	EFPC	OO	
43122		**FB**	FG	EFPC	OO	
43124		**FB**	A	EFPC	LE	
43125		**FB**	A	EFPC	LE	
43126		**FB**	A	EFPC	LE	
43127		**FB**	A	EFPC	LE	Sir Peter Parker 1924–2002 Cotswold Line 150
43128		**FB**	A	EFPC	LE	
43129		**FB**	A	EFPC	LE	
43130		**FB**	A	EFPC	LE	
43131		**FB**	A	EFPC	LE	
43132		**FB**	A	EFPC	LE	We Save the Children – Will You?
43133		**FB**	A	EFPC	LE	
43134		**FB**	A	EFPC	LE	
43135		**FB**	A	EFPC	LE	
43136		**FB**	A	EFPC	LE	
43137		**FB**	A	EFPC	LE	Newton Abbot 150
43138		**FB**	A	EFPC	LE	Driver Stan Martin
43139		**FB**	A	EFPC	LE	25 June 1950 – 6 November 2004
43140		**FB**	A	EFPC	LE	
43141		**FB**	A	EFPC	LE	
43142		**FB**	A	EFPC	LE	Reading Panel Signal Box 1965–2010
43143		**FB**	A	EFPC	LE	Stroud 700
43144		**FB**	A	EFPC	LE	
43145		**FB**	A	EFPC	LE	
43146		**FB**	A	EFPC	LE	
43147		**FB**	A	EFPC	LE	
43148		**FB**	A	EFPC	LE	
43149		**FB**	A	EFPC	LE	University of Plymouth
43150		**FB**	A	EFPC	LE	

43151	**FB**	A	EFPC	LE	
43152	**FB**	A	EFPC	LE	
43153	**FB**	FG	EFPC	OO	
43154	**FB**	FG	EFPC	OO	
43155	**FB**	FG	EFPC	OO	
43156	**FB**	P	EFPC	OO	Dartington International Summer School
43158	**FB**	FG	EFPC	OO	
43159	**FB**	P	EFPC	OO	
43160	**FB**	P	EFPC	OO	Sir Moir Lockhead OBE
43161	**FB**	P	EFPC	OO	
43162	**FB**	P	EFPC	OO	
43163	**FB**	A	EFPC	OO	Exeter Panel Signal Box 21st Anniversary 2009
43164	**FB**	A	EFPC	OO	
43165	**FB**	A	EFPC	OO	Prince Michael of Kent
43168	**FB**	A	EFPC	OO	THE NATIONAL TRUST
43169	**FB**	A	EFPC	OO	
43170	**FB**	A	EFPC	OO	
43171	**FB**	A	EFPC	OO	
43172	**FB**	A	EFPC	OO	
43174	**FB**	A	EFPC	OO	
43175	**FB**	A	EFPC	OO	GWR 175TH ANNIVERSARY
43176	**FB**	A	EFPC	OO	
43177	**FB**	A	EFPC	OO	
43179	**FB**	A	EFPC	OO	Pride of Laira
43180	**FB**	P	EFPC	OO	
43181	**FB**	A	EFPC	OO	
43182	**FB**	A	EFPC	OO	
43183	**FB**	A	EFPC	OO	
43185	**FB**	A	EFPC	OO	Great Western
43186	**FB**	A	EFPC	OO	
43187	**FB**	A	EFPC	OO	
43188	**FB**	A	EFPC	OO	
43189	**FB**	A	EFPC	OO	RAILWAY HERITAGE TRUST
43190	**FB**	A	EFPC	OO	
43191	**FB**	A	EFPC	OO	
43192	**FB**	A	EFPC	OO	
43193	**FB**	P	EFPC	OO	
43194	**FB**	FG	EFPC	OO	
43195	**FB**	P	EFPC	OO	
43196	**FB**	P	EFPC	OO	
43197	**FB**	P	EFPC	OO	
43198	**FB**	FG	EFPC	OO	Oxfordshire 2007

Class 43/2. Rebuilt East Coast, CrossCountry and Grand Central power cars.
Power cars have been renumbered by adding 200 to their original number or 400 to their original number except 43123 which became 43423.

43206	(43006)	**EC** A	IECP	EC	
43207	(43007)	**XC** A	EHPC	EC	
43208	(43008)	**NX** A	IECP	EC	Lincolnshire Echo
43238	(43038)	**NX** A	IECP	EC	

43239 (43039)	**NX**	A	IECP	EC	
43251 (43051)	**EC**	P	IECP	EC	
43257 (43057)	**NX**	P	IECP	EC	
43272 (43072)	**EC**	P	IECP	EC	
43274 (43074)	**EC**	P	IECP	EC	
43277 (43077)	**EC**	P	IECP	EC	
43285 (43085)	**XC**	P	EHPC	EC	
43290 (43090)	**EC**	P	IECP	EC	mtu fascination of power
43295 (43095)	**EC**	A	IECP	EC	
43296 (43096)	**EC**	A	IECP	EC	
43299 (43099)	**NX**	P	IECP	EC	
43300 (43100)	**EC**	P	IECP	EC	Craigentinny
43301 (43101)	**XC**	P	EHPC	EC	
43302 (43102)	**EC**	P	IECP	EC	
43303 (43103)	**XC**	P	EHPC	EC	
43304 (43104)	**XC**	A	EHPC	EC	
43305 (43105)	**NX**	A	IECP	EC	
43306 (43106)	**NX**	A	IECP	EC	
43307 (43107)	**EC**	A	IECP	EC	
43308 (43108)	**EC**	A	IECP	EC	
43309 (43109)	**EC**	A	IECP	EC	
43310 (43110)	**NX**	A	IECP	EC	
43311 (43111)	**EC**	A	IECP	EC	
43312 (43112)	**NX**	A	IECP	EC	
43313 (43113)	**NX**	A	IECP	EC	
43314 (43114)	**EC**	A	IECP	EC	
43315 (43115)	**EC**	A	IECP	EC	
43316 (43116)	**EC**	A	IECP	EC	
43317 (43117)	**NX**	A	IECP	EC	
43318 (43118)	**NX**	A	IECP	EC	
43319 (43119)	**EC**	A	IECP	EC	
43320 (43120)	**NX**	A	IECP	EC	
43321 (43121)	**XC**	P	EHPC	EC	
43357 (43157)	**XC**	P	EHPC	EC	
43366 (43166)	**XC**	A	EHPC	EC	
43367 (43167)	**NX**	A	IECP	EC	DELTIC 50 1955–2005
43378 (43178)	**XC**	A	EHPC	EC	
43384 (43184)	**XC**	A	EHPC	EC	'VALENTA' 1972–2010
43423 (43123) †	**GC**	A	GCHP	HT	
43465 (43065) †	**GC**	A	GCHP	HT	
43467 (43067) †	**GC**	A	GCHP	HT	
43468 (43068) †	**GC**	A	GCHP	HT	
43480 (43080) †	**GC**	A	GCHP	HT	
43484 (43084) †	**GC**	A	GCHP	HT	PETER FOX 1942–2011
					PLATFORM 5

CLASS 47   BR/BRUSH/SULZER   Co-Co

Built: 1963–67 by Brush Traction, at Loughborough or by BR at Crewe Works.
Engine: Sulzer 12LDA28C of 1920 kW (2580 hp) at 750 rpm.
Main Generator: Brush TG160-60 Mk4 or TM172-50 Mk1.
Traction Motors: Brush TM64-68 Mk1 or Mk1A.
Maximum Tractive Effort: 267 kN (60000 lbf).
Continuous Tractive Effort: 133 kN (30000 lbf) at 26 mph.
Power At Rail: 1550 kW (2080 hp).   **Train Brakes:** Air.
Brake Force: 61 t.   **Dimensions:** 19.38 x 2.79 m.
Weight: 111.5–120.6 t.   **Wheel Diameter:** 1143 mm.
Design Speed: 95 mph.
Maximum Speed: 95 mph (* 75 mph).
Fuel Capacity: 3273 (+ 5887).   **RA:** 6 or 7.
Train Supply: Not equipped.
Multiple Working: m Green Circle (operational locos only).

Originally numbered in series D1100–D1111, D1500–D1999 but not in order.

Non-standard liveries/numbering:

47270	Also carries number D1971.
47773	Also carries number D1755.
47812	Also carries number D1916.
47815	Also carries number D1748.
47829	"Police" livery of white with a broad red band outlined in yellow.

Class 47/0 (Dual-braked locos) or Class 47/2 (Air-braked locos). Standard Design. Details as above.

47194 a+	**F**	WC	MBDL	CS (S)	
47236 +	**FE**	WC	MBDL	CS (S)	
47237 x+	**WC**	WC	MBDL	CS	
47245 x+m	**WC**	WC	MBDL	CS	
47270 a+	**B**	PO	MBDL	CS	SWIFT

Class 47/3 (Dual-braked locos) or Class 47/2 (Air-braked locos).
Details as Class 47/0 except: **Weight:** 113.7 t.

47355 am+	**WC**	WC	MBDL	CS (S)
47368 x	**F**	WC	MBDL	CS (S)
47375 +m	**B**	NS	NRLO	BO

Class 47/4. Electric Train Supply equipment.
Details as Class 47/0 except:

Weight: 120.4–125.1 t.   **Fuel Capacity:** 3273 (+ 5537) litres.
Train Supply: Electric. ETH 66.   **RA:** 7.

47492 x	**RX**	WC	MBDL	CS (S)	
47500 x	**WC**	WC	MBDL	CS	
47501 xm+	**DS**	DR	XHAC	KM	Craftsman
47526 x	**BL**	WC	MBDL	CS (S)	
47580 x	**BL**	47	MBDL	TM	County of Essex

Class 47/7. Previously fitted with an older form of TDM.

Details as Class 47/4 except:
Weight: 118.7 t.   **Fuel Capacity:** 5887 litres.
Maximum Speed: 100 mph.

47712	xm	**DS**	DR	XHSS	CP (S)	Pride of Carlisle

Class 47/7. Former Railnet dedicated locos. All have twin fuel tanks.

47727	m	**CS**	CS	COLO	WH	Rebecca
47739	m	**CS**	CS	COLO	WH	Robin of Templecombe
47746		**RX**	WC	MBDL	CS (S)	
47747		**E**	DR	XHHP	CR (S)	
47749	m	**CS**	CS	COLO	WH	Demelza
47760	x	**WC**	WC	MBDL	CS	
47768		**RX**	WC	MBDL	CS (S)	
47769		**V**	RV	RTLO	CP	Resolve
47772	x	**RX**	WC	MBDL	CS (S)	
47773	x	**GG**	70	MBDL	TM	
47776	x	**RX**	WC	MBDL	CS (S)	
47786		**WC**	WC	MBDL	CS	Roy Castle OBE
47787		**WC**	WC	MBDL	CS (S)	Windsor Castle
47790	m	**VN**	DR	XHAC	KM	Galloway Princess
47791		**DR**	DR	XHHP	BH (S)	

Class 47/4 continued. RA6. Most fitted with extended-range fuel tanks (+).

47798	x	**RP**	NM	MBDL	YK	Prince William
47802	+m	**DS**	DR	XHAC	KM	Pride of Cumbria
47804		**WC**	WC	MBDL	CS	
47805	+m	**DS**	DR	XHAC	KM	
47810	+m	**DS**	DR	XHAC	KM	Peter Bath MBE 1927–2006
47811	+	**GL**	FL	DFLH	BA	
47812	+m	**GG**	RV	RTLO	CP	Solent
47813	+m	**DS**	DR	XHAC	KM	Solent
47815	+m	**GG**	RV	RTLO	CP	GREAT WESTERN
47816	+	**GL**	FL	DFLH	BA (S)	
47818	+m	**DS**	DR	XHAC	KM	
47826	+	**WC**	WC	MBDL	CS	
47828	+m	**DS**	DR	XHAC	KM	
47829	+	**O**	HN	HNRS	LM (S)	
47830	+	**GL**	FL	DFLH	BH (S)	Solway Princess
47832	+m	**VN**	DR	XHAC	KM	Solway Princess
47839	+m	**RV**	DR	XHHP	ZG (S)	
47841	+m	**DS**	DR	XHAC	KM	
47843	+m	**RV**	RV	RTLO	CP	VULCAN
47847	+m	**BL**	RV	RTLO	CP	
47848	+m	**RV**	RV	RTLO	CP	TITAN STAR
47851	+	**WC**	WC	MBDL	CS	RAIL EXPRESS
47853	+m	**DS**	DR	XHAC	KM	RAIL EXPRESS
47854	+	**WC**	WC	MBDL	CS	Diamond Jubilee

CLASS 50   ENGLISH ELECTRIC   Co-Co

Built: 1967–68 by English Electric at Vulcan Foundry, Newton-le-Willows.
Engine: English Electric 16CVST of 2010 kW (2700 hp) at 850 rpm.
Main Generator: English Electric 840/4B.
Traction Motors: English Electric 538/5A.
Maximum Tractive Effort: 216 kN (48500 lbf).
Continuous Tractive Effort: 147 kN (33000 lbf) at 23.5 mph.
Power At Rail: 1540 kW (2070 hp).   **Train Brakes:** Air & vacuum.
Brake Force: 59 t.   **Dimensions:** 20.88 x 2.78 m.
Weight: 116.9 t.   **Wheel Diameter:** 1092 mm.
Design Speed: 105 mph.   **Maximum Speed:** 90 mph.
Fuel Capacity: 4796 litres.   **RA:** 6.
Train Supply: Electric, index 61.   **Multiple Working:** Orange Square.

Originally numbered D444 & D449.

50044	**B**	50	CFOL		KR	Exeter
50049	**BL**	50	CFOL		KR	Defiance

CLASS 52   BR/MAYBACH   C-C

Built: 1961–64 by BR at Swindon Works.
Engine: Two Maybach MD655 of 1007 kW (1350 hp) at 1500 rpm.
Transmission: Hydraulic. Voith L630rV.
Maximum Tractive Effort: 297 kN (66700 lbf).
Continuous Tractive Effort: 201 kN (45200 lbf) at 14.5 mph.
Power At Rail: 1490 kW (2000 hp).   **Train Brakes:** Air & vacuum.
Brake Force: 83 t.   **Dimensions:** 20.7 m x 2.78 m.
Weight: 110 t.   **Wheel Diameter:** 1092 mm.
Design Speed: 90 mph.   **Maximum Speed:** 90 mph.
Fuel Capacity: 3900 litres.   **RA:** 6.
Train Supply: Steam.   **Multiple Working:** Not equipped.

Never allocated a number in the 1972 number series.

Registered on TOPS as No. 89416.

D1015	**M**	DT	MBDL		TM	WESTERN CHAMPION

CLASS 55   ENGLISH ELECTRIC   Co-Co

Built: 1961 by English Electric at Vulcan Foundry, Newton-le-Willows.
Engine: Two Napier-Deltic D18-25 of 1230 kW (1650 hp) each at 1500 rpm.
Main Generators: Two English Electric 829/1A.
Traction Motors: English Electric 538/A.
Maximum Tractive Effort: 222 kN (50000 lbf).
Continuous Tractive Effort: 136 kN (30500 lbf) at 32.5 mph.
Power At Rail: 1969 kW (2640 hp).   **Train Brakes:** Air & vacuum.
Brake Force: 51 t.   **Dimensions:** 21.18 x 2.68 m.
Weight: 100 t.   **Wheel Diameter:** 1092 mm.
Design Speed: 105 mph.   **Maximum Speed:** 100 mph.

Fuel Capacity: 3755 litres. **RA:** 5.
Train Supply: Electric, index 66. **Multiple Working:** Not equipped.

Originally numbered D9002, D9009 & D9000.

55022 registered on TOPS as No. 89500.

55002	B	NM	MBDL	YK	THE KING'S OWN YORKSHIRE LIGHT INFANTRY
55009	GG	DP	MBDL	BQ	ALYCIDON
55022	B	MW	ELRD	BQ	ROYAL SCOTS GREY

55019

CLASS 56   BRUSH/BR/RUSTON   Co-Co

Built: 1976–84 by Electroputere at Craiova, Romania (as sub contractors for Brush) or BREL at Doncaster or Crewe Works.
Engine: Ruston Paxman 16RK3CT of 2460 kW (3250 hp) at 900 rpm.
Main Alternator: Brush BA1101A.
Traction Motors: Brush TM73-62.
Maximum Tractive Effort: 275 kN (61800 lbf).
Continuous Tractive Effort: 240 kN (53950 lbf) at 16.8 mph.
Power At Rail: 1790 kW (2400 hp). **Train Brakes:** Air.
Brake Force: 60 t. **Dimensions:** 19.36 x 2.79 m.
Weight: 126 t. **Wheel Diameter:** 1143 mm.
Design Speed: 80 mph. **Maximum Speed:** 80 mph.
Fuel Capacity: 5228 litres. **RA:** 7.
Train Supply: Not equipped. **Multiple Working:** Red Diamond.

Note: All equipped with Slow Speed Control.

Non-standard liveries:

56311 and 56312 Light grey with yellow cabsides.

56006	B	X	WNSO	BH (S)
56007	FER	ED	NRHL	BO (S)
56018	FER	ZW	NRHL	BO (S)
56037	E	X	WNSO	CD (S)
56051	FER	ZW	NRHL	BO (S)
56060	FER	ZW	NRHL	BO (S)
56065	FER	ED	NRHL	BO (S)
56077	LH	X	WNSO	CD (S)
56078	FER	CS	COLO	RU (S)
56081	FER	ZW	NRHL	BO (S)
56086	BL	EP	EPXX	WH (S)
56087	CS	CS	COLO	WH
56091	FER	BA	HTLX	WH
56094	CS	CS	COLO	WH
56096	FER	EP	EPXX	WH (S)
56103	FER	BA	HTLX	WH (S)
56105	FER	CS	COLO	WH (S)
56113	FER	CS	COLO	WH (S)
56128	F	BA	HTLX	WF (S)

56301 (56045)	**FA**	56	NRHL	WH
56302 (56124)	**FA**	ED	NRHL	WH
56303 (56125)	**DC**	BA	HTLX	WH
56311 (56057)	**0**	BA	HTLX	WH
56312 (56003)	**0**	BA	HTLX	WH

CLASS 57   BRUSH/GM   Co-Co

Built: 1964–65 by Brush Traction at Loughborough or BR at Crewe Works as Class 47. Rebuilt 1997–2004 by Brush Traction at Loughborough.
Engine: General Motors 12 645 E3 of 1860 kW (2500 hp) at 904 rpm.
Main Alternator: Brush BA1101D.
Traction Motors: Brush TM64-68 Mark 1 or Mark 1a.
Maximum Tractive Effort: 244.5 kN (55000 lbf).
Continuous Tractive Effort: 140 kN (31500 lbf) at ?? mph.
Power at Rail: 1507 kW (2025 hp).   **Train Brakes:** Air.
Brake Force: 80 t.   **Dimensions:** 19.38 x 2.79 m.
Weight: 120.6 t.   **Wheel Diameter:** 1143 mm.
Design Speed: 75 mph.   **Maximum Speed:** 75 mph.
Fuel Capacity: 5550 litres.   **RA:** 6
Train Supply: Not equipped.   **Multiple Working:** † DRS system.

Class 57/0. No Train Supply Equipment. Rebuilt 1997–2000.

57001 (47356)	**WC**	WC	MBDL	CS
57002 (47322) †	**DS**	P	XHCK	KM
57003 (47317) †	**DS**	P	XHCK	KM
57004 (47347) †	**DS**	DR	XHCK	KM
57005 (47350)	**AZ**	WC	MBDL	CS (S)
57006 (47187)	**WC**	WC	MBDL	CS
57007 (47332) †	**DS**	P	XHCK	KM
57008 (47060) †	**DS**	P	XHCK	KM	Telford International Railfreight Park June 2009
57009 (47079) †	**DS**	P	XHCK	KM
57010 (47231) †	**DS**	P	XHSS	ZG (S)
57011 (47329) †	**DS**	P	XHCK	KM
57012 (47204) †	**DS**	P	XHSS	ZA (S)

Class 57/3. Electric Train Supply Equipment. Virgin Trains locos. Rebuilt 2002–04. Details as Class 57/0 except:

Engine: General Motors 12645F3B of 2050 kW (2750 hp) at 954 rpm.
Main Alternator: Brush BA1101F (recovered from a Class 56) or Brush BA1101G.
Fuel Capacity: 5887 litres.   **Train Supply:** Electric, index 100.
Design Speed: 95 mph.   **Maximum Speed:** 95 mph.
Brake Force: 60 t.   **Weight:** 117 t.

Non-standard livery: 57313 & 57316 All over blue.

57301 (47845) d	**Y**	P	QADD	ZG	
57302 (47827) d	**DS**	P	XHAC	KM	Chad Varah
57303 (47705) d	**Y**	P	QADD	ZG	
57304 (47807) d	**DS**	P	XHAC	KM	Pride of Cheshire

57305	(47822) d	**Y**	P	QADD	ZG	
57306	(47814) d	**Y**	P	QADD	ZG	
57307	(47225) d	**VT**	P	IWCA	MA	LADY PENELOPE
57308	(47846) d	**VT**	P	IWCA	MA	TIN TIN
57309	(47806) d	**DS**	P	XHAC	KM	Pride of Crewe
57310	(47831) d	**Y**	P	QADD	ZG	
57311	(47817) d	**VT**	P	IWCA	MA	PARKER
57312	(47730) d	**Y**	P	QADD	ZG	Peter Henderson
57313	(47371) d	**0**	P	IWCA	MA	
57314	(47372) d	**AB**	P	IWCA	MA	
57315	(47234) d	**AB**	P	IWCA	MA	
57316	(47290) d	**0**	P	IWCA	MA	

Class 57/6. Electric Train Supply Equipment. Prototype ETS loco. Rebuilt 2001. Details as Class 57/0 except:

Main Alternator: Brush BA1101E.	**Fuel Capacity:** 3273 litres.
Train Supply: Electric, index 95.	**Weight:** 113t.
Design Speed: 95 mph.	**Maximum Speed:** 95 mph.
Brake Force: 60 t.	

57601	(47825)	**WC**	WC	MBDL	CS

Class 57/6. Electric Train Supply Equipment. First Great Western locos. Rebuilt 2004. Details as Class 57/3.

57602	(47337)	**FB**	P	EFOO	OO	Restormel Castle
57603	(47349)	**FB**	P	EFOO	OO	Tintagel Castle
57604	(47209)	**GW**	P	EFOO	OO	PENDENNIS CASTLE
57605	(47206)	**FB**	P	EFOO	OO	Totnes Castle

CLASS 58   BREL/RUSTON   Co-Co

Built: 1983–87 by BREL at Doncaster Works.
Engine: Ruston Paxman 12RK3ACT of 2460 kW (3300 hp) at 1000 rpm.
Main Alternator: Brush BA1101B.   **Traction Motors:** Brush TM73-62.
Maximum Tractive Effort: 275 kN (61800 lbf).
Continuous Tractive Effort: 240 kN (53950 lbf) at 17.4 mph.

Power At Rail: 1780 kW (2387 hp).	**Train Brakes:** Air.
Brake Force: 60 t.	**Dimensions:** 19.13 x 2.72 m.
Weight: 130 t.	**Wheel Diameter:** 1120 mm.
Design Speed: 80 mph.	**Maximum Speed:** 80 mph.
Fuel Capacity: 4214 litres.	**RA:** 7.
Train Supply: Not equipped.	**Multiple Working:** Red Diamond.

Notes: All equipped with Slow Speed Control.

Class 58s exported for use abroad are listed in section 6 of this book.

58002	**ML**	DB	WNSQ	EH (S)
58008	**ML**	DB	WNTS	EH (S)
58012	**F**	DB	WNTS	TO (S)
58017	**F**	DB	WNXX	EH (S)
58022	**F**	DB	WNTS	CD (S)

58023	**ML**	DB	WNTS	TO (S)
58037	**E**	DB	WNXX	EH (S)
58048	**E**	DB	WNTS	CE (S)

CLASS 59   GENERAL MOTORS   Co-Co

Built: 1985 (59001/002/004) or 1989 (59005) by General Motors, La Grange, Illinois, USA or 1990 (59101–104), 1994 (59201) and 1995 (59202–206) by General Motors, London, Ontario, Canada.
Engine: General Motors 16-645E3C two stroke of 2460 kW (3300 hp) at 904 rpm.
Main Alternator: General Motors AR11 MLD-D14A.
Traction Motors: General Motors D77B.
Maximum Tractive Effort: 506 kN (113 550 lbf).
Continuous Tractive Effort: 291 kN (65 300 lbf) at 14.3 mph.
Power At Rail: 1889 kW (2533 hp).   **Train Brakes:** Air.
Brake Force: 69 t.
Weight: 121 t.   **Dimensions:** 21.35 x 2.65 m.
Wheel Diameter: 1067 mm.
Design Speed: 60 (* 75) mph.   **Maximum Speed:** 60 (* 75) mph.
Fuel Capacity: 4546 litres.   **RA:** 7.
Train Supply: Not equipped.   **Multiple Working:** AAR System.

Class 59/0. Owned by Aggregate Industries.

59001	**AI**	AI	XYPO	MD	YEOMAN ENDEAVOUR
59002	**FY**	AI	XYPO	MD	ALAN J DAY
59004	**FY**	AI	XYPO	MD	PAUL A HAMMOND
59005	**AI**	AI	XYPO	MD	KENNETH J PAINTER

Class 59/1. Owned by Hanson Quarry Products.

59101	**HA**	HA	XYPA	MD	Village of Whatley
59102	**HA**	HA	XYPA	MD	Village of Chantry
59103	**HA**	HA	XYPA	MD	Village of Mells
59104	**HA**	HA	XYPA	MD	Village of Great Elm

Class 59/2. Owned by DB Schenker.

59201	*	**DB**	DB	WDAK	MD	
59202	*	**DB**	DB	WDAK	MD	
59203	*	**DB**	DB	WDAK	MD	
59204	*	**DB**	DB	WDAK	MD	
59205	*b	**DB**	DB	WDAK	MD	
59206	*b	**DB**	DB	WNWX	LT (S)	John F. Yeoman Rail Pioneer

CLASS 60   BRUSH/MIRRLEES   Co-Co

Built: 1989–93 by Brush Traction at Loughborough.
Engine: Mirrlees 8MB275T of 2310 kW (3100 hp) at 1000 rpm.
Main Alternator: Brush BA1006A.
Traction Motors: Brush TM2161A.
Maximum Tractive Effort: 500 kN (106500 lbf).
Continuous Tractive Effort: 336 kN (71570 lbf) at 17.4 mph.
Power At Rail: 1800 kW (2415 hp).   **Train Brakes:** Air.
Brake Force: 74 (+ 62) t.   **Dimensions:** 21.34 x 2.64 m.
Weight: 129 (+ 131) t.   **Wheel Diameter:** 1118 mm.
Design Speed: 62 mph.   **Maximum Speed:** 60 mph.
Fuel Capacity: 4546 (+ 5225) litres. **RA:** 8.
Train Supply: Not equipped.   **Multiple Working:** Within class.

Important note, DB Schenker Fleet Management Unit: As all operational
Class 60s are effectively treated as "common user" by DB Schenker, and
allocated to operational pools depending on which duties they are on at
the time, all operational locos are shown in the WFMU Fleet Management
pool here. Details of the other individual pools can be found in the codes
section of this book.

Notes: All equipped with Slow Speed Control.

* Refurbished locos.

60034, 60064, 60066, 60072, 60073, 60077, 60082, 60084 and 60090 carry
their names on one side only.

60500 originally carried the number 60016.

Advertising/promotional liveries:

60074 Teenage Cancer Trust (light blue).
60099 Tata Steel (silver).

60001	E	DB	WNWX	TO (S)	The Railway Observer
60002	+ E	DB	WNTS	CD (S)	High Peak
60003	+ E	DB	WNTS	TO (S)	FREIGHT TRANSPORT ASSOCIATION
60004	+ E	DB	WNTS	TO (S)	
60005	+ E	DB	WNTS	TO (S)	
60006	CU	DB	WNTS	TO (S)	
60007	+* DB	DB	WFMU	TO	The Spirit of Tom Kendell
60008	E	DB	WNTS	TO (S)	Sir William McAlpine
60009	+ E	DB	WNTS	TO (S)	
60010	+* DB	DB	WFMU	TO	
60011	DB	DB	WFMU	TO	
60012	+ E	DB	WNWX	TO (S)	Robert Boyle
60013	EG	DB	WNTS	TO (S)	
60014	EG	DB	WNTS	TO (S)	
60015	+* DB	DB	WFMU	TO	
60017	+* DB	DB	WFMU	TO	
60018	E	DB	WNTS	TO (S)	
60019	* DB	DB	WFMU	TO	Port of Grimsby & Immingham

60020 +	E	DB	WNWX	TO (S)	
60021 +	E	DB	WNTS	TO (S)	
60022 +	E	DB	WNTS	TO (S)	
60023 +	E	DB	WNTS	TO (S)	
60024	E	DB	WFMU	TO	
60025 +	E	DB	WNTS	TO (S)	
60026 +	E	DB	WNTS	TO (S)	
60027 +	E	DB	WNTS	TO (S)	
60028 +	EG	DB	WNTS	CD (S)	John Flamsteed
60029	E	DB	WNTS	CD (S)	Clitheroe Castle
60030 +	E	DB	WNTS	TO (S)	
60031	E	DB	WNTS	TO (S)	
60032	F	DB	WNTS	TO (S)	
60033 +	CU	DB	WNWX	TO (S)	Tees Steel Express
60034	EG	DB	WNTS	TO (S)	Carnedd Llewelyn
60035	E	DB	WFMU	TO	
60036	E	DB	WNTS	TO (S)	GEFCO
60037 +	E	DB	WNTS	TO (S)	
60038 +	E	DB	WNTS	CD (S)	AvestaPolarit
60039	E	DB	WNWX	TO (S)	
60040 *	DB	DB	WFMU	TO	The Territorial Army Centenary
60041 +	E	DB	WNTS	TO (S)	
60042	E	DB	WNTS	TO (S)	
60043	E	DB	WNWX	TO (S)	
60044	ML	DB	WNWX	BZ (S)	
60045	E	DB	WFMU	TO	The Permanent Way Institution
60046 +	EG	DB	WNTS	CD (S)	William Wilberforce
60047	E	DB	WNTS	CD (S)	
60048	E	DB	WNTS	TO (S)	
60049	E	DB	WFMU	TO	
60050	E	DB	WNTS	TO (S)	
60051 +	E	DB	WNTS	TO (S)	
60052 +	E	DB	WNTS	TO (S)	Glofa Twr – The last deep mine in Wales – Tower Colliery
60053	E	DB	WNTS	TO (S)	
60054 +*	DB	DB	WFMU	TO	
60055 +	EG	DB	WNTS	CD (S)	Thomas Barnardo
60056 +	EG	DB	WNTS	CD (S)	William Beveridge
60057	EG	DB	WNTS	TO (S)	Adam Smith
60058 +	E	DB	WNTS	TO (S)	
60059 +*	DB	DB	WFMU	TO	Swinden Dalesman
60060	EG	DB	WNTS	TO (S)	
60061	F	DB	WNTS	TO (S)	
60062	E	DB	WNTR	TO (S)	
60063 *	DB	DB	WFMU	TO	
60064 +	EG	DB	WNTS	TO (S)	Back Tor
60065	E	DB	WFMU	TO	Spirit of JAGUAR
60066	EG	DB	WNTS	TO (S)	John Logie Baird
60067	EG	DB	WNTS	TO (S)	
60068	EG	DB	WNTS	TO (S)	
60069	E	DB	WNTS	TO (S)	Slioch

60070	+	F	DB	WNTS	TO (S) John Loudon McAdam
60071	+	E	DB	WNTR	TO Ribblehead Viaduct
60072		EG	DB	WNTS	TO (S) Cairn Toul
60073		EG	DB	WNTS	TO (S) Cairn Gorm
60074	*	AL	DB	WFMU	TO Teenage Spirit
60075		E	DB	WNTS	TO (S)
60076		EG	DB	WNTS	CD (S)
60077	+	EG	DB	WNTS	TO (S) Canisp
60078		ML	DB	WNTS	TO (S)
60079	*	DB	DB	WFMU	TO
60080	+	E	DB	WNTS	TO (S)
60081	+	GW	DB	WNTS	TO (S)
60082		EG	DB	WNTS	CD (S) Mam Tor
60083		E	DB	WNTS	TO (S)
60084		EG	DB	WNTS	TO (S) Cross Fell
60085		E	DB	WNTS	TO (S) MINI Pride of Oxford
60086		EG	DB	WNTS	TO (S)
60087		E	DB	WNWX	TO (S)
60088		F	DB	WNTS	TO (S)
60089	+	E	DB	WNTS	TO (S)
60090	+	EG	DB	WNTS	TO (S) Quinag
60091	+*	DB	DB	WFMU	TO
60092	+	EG	DB	WNWX	TO (S) Reginald Munns
60093		E	DB	WNTS	TO (S)
60094		E	DB	WNTS	TO (S) Rugby Flyer
60095		EG	DB	WNTS	CD (S)
60096	+	E	DB	WNTS	BZ (S)
60097	+	E	DB	WNTS	TO (S)
60098	+	E	DB	WNTS	TO (S)
60099		AL	DB	WFMU	TO
60100		E	DB	WNWX	BZ (S)
60500		E	DB	WNTS	TO (S)

CLASS 66   GENERAL MOTORS/EMD   Co-Co

Built: 1998–2008 by General Motors/EMD, London, Ontario, Canada (Model JT42CWR (low emission locos Model JT42CWRM)).
Engine: General Motors 12N-710G3B-EC two stroke of 2385 kW (3200 hp) at 904 rpm.
Main Alternator: General Motors AR8/CA6.
Traction Motors: General Motors D43TR.
Maximum Tractive Effort: 409 kN (92000 lbf).
Continuous Tractive Effort: 260 kN (58390 lbf) at 15.9 mph.

Power At Rail: 1850 kW (2480 hp).	**Train Brakes:** Air.
Brake Force: 68 t.	**Dimensions:** 21.35 x 2.64 m.
Weight: 127 t.	**Wheel Diameter:** 1120 mm.
Design Speed: 87.5 mph.	**Maximum Speed:** 75 mph (* 60 mph).
Fuel Capacity: 6550 litres.	**RA:** 7.
Train Supply: Not equipped.	**Multiple Working:** AAR System.

Important note, DB Schenker Fleet Management Unit: As all DB Schenker Class 66s are effectively now treated as "common user" by DB Schenker, and allocated to operational pools depending on which duties they are on at the time, all operational locos are shown in the WFMU Fleet Management pool here. Details of the other individual pools can be found in the codes section of this book.

Notes: All equipped with Slow Speed Control.

Class 66s previously used in the UK but now in use abroad are listed in section 6 of this book. Some of the 60 DBS 66s moved to France return to Great Britain from time to time according to operational requirements, those working in Britain at the time of writing are shown with a *.

Advertising livery: 66048 Stobart Rail (two tone blue & white).

Class 66 delivery dates. The Class 66 design evolved over a 10-year period with over 400 delivered. For clarity the delivery dates (by year) for each batch of locos is as follows:

66001–66250	EWS (now DB Schenker). 1998–2000 (some now in use in France or Poland).
66301–66305	Fastline. 2008. Now used by DRS.
66401–66410	DRS. 2003. Now in use with GB Railfreight or Colas Rail and renumbered 66733–737 and 66742–746.
66411–66420	DRS. 2006. Now leased by Freightliner (66411/417 exported to Poland).
66421–66430	DRS. 2007
66431–66434	DRS. 2008
66501–66505	Freightliner. 1999
66506–66520	Freightliner. 2000
66521–66525	Freightliner. 2000 (66521 since scrapped).
66526–66531	Freightliner. 2001
66532–66537	Freightliner. 2001
66538–66543	Freightliner. 2001
66544–66553	Freightliner. 2001
66554	Freightliner. 2002†
66555–66566	Freightliner. 2002
66567–66574	Freightliner. 2003. 66573–574 now used by Colas Rail and renumbered 66846–847.
66575–66577	Freightliner. 2004. Now used by Colas Rail and renumbered 66848–850.
66578–66581	Freightliner. 2005. Now used by GBRf and renumbered 66738–741.
66582–66594	Freightliner. 2007 (66582/583/584/586 exported to Poland).
66595–66599	Freightliner. 2008
66601–66606	Freightliner. 2000
66607–66612	Freightliner. 2002 (66607/609/611/612 exported to Poland)
66613–66618	Freightliner. 2003
66619–66622	Freightliner. 2005
66623–66625	Freightliner. 2007 (66624/625 exported to Poland).
66701–66707	GB Railfreight. 2001
66708–66712	GB Railfreight. 2002

66713–66717	GB Railfreight. 2003
66718–66722	GB Railfreight. 2006
66723–66727	GB Railfreight. 2006
66728–66732	GB Railfreight. 2008
66951–66952	Freightliner. 2004
66953–66957	Freightliner. 2008

† Replacement for 66521, written off in the Great Heck accident in 2001.

Class 66/0. DB Schenker-operated locos.

Notes: All fitted with Swinghead Automatic "Buckeye" Combination Couplers except 66001 and 66002.

† Fitted with additional lights and drawgear for Lickey banking duties.

* Locos originally modified for use in France and returned to Britain. Maximum speed 60 mph.

t Fitted with tripcocks for working over London Underground tracks between Harrow-on-the-Hill and Amersham.

66001 t	E	A	WFMU	TO	
66002	E	A	WFMU	TO	Lafarge Quorn
66003	E	A	WFMU	TO	
66004	E	A	WFMU	TO	
66005	E	A	WFMU	TO	
66006	E	A	WFMU	TO	
66007	E	A	WFMU	TO	
66008	E	A	WFMU	TO	
66009	E	A	WFMU	TO	
66010 *	E	A	WBES	TO	
66011	E	A	WFMU	TO	
66012	E	A	WFMU	TO	
66013	E	A	WFMU	TO	
66014	E	A	WFMU	TO	
66015	E	A	WFMU	TO	
66016	E	A	WFMU	TO	
66017 t	E	A	WFMU	TO	
66018	E	A	WFMU	TO	
66019 t	E	A	WFMU	TO	
66020	E	A	WFMU	TO	
66021	E	A	WFMU	TO	
66023	E	A	WFMU	TO	
66024	E	A	WFMU	TO	
66025	E	A	WFMU	TO	
66027	E	A	WFMU	TO	
66030	E	A	WFMU	TO	
66031	E	A	WFMU	TO	
66033 *	E	A	WBEN	TO	
66034	E	A	WFMU	TO	
66035	E	A	WFMU	TO	
66037	E	A	WFMU	TO	
66039	E	A	WFMU	TO	
66040	E	A	WFMU	TO	

66041	E	A	WFMU	TO	
66042 *	E	A	WBES	TO	
66043	E	A	WFMU	TO	
66044	E	A	WFMU	TO	
66045 *	E	A	WBES	TO	
66046	E	A	WFMU	TO	
66047	E	A	WFMU	TO	
66048	AL	A	WNTS	TO (S)	James the Engine
66050	E	A	WFMU	TO	EWS Energy
66051	E	A	WFMU	TO	
66052 *	E	A	WBES	TO	
66053	E	A	WFMU	TO	
66054	E	A	WFMU	TO	
66055 †	E	A	WFMU	TO	
66056 †	E	A	WFMU	TO	
66057 †	E	A	WFMU	TO	
66058 †	E	A	WFMU	TO	
66059 †	E	A	WFMU	TO	
66060	E	A	WFMU	TO	
66061	E	A	WFMU	TO	
66062 *	E	A	WBES	TO	
66063	E	A	WFMU	TO	
66065	E	A	WFMU	TO	
66066	E	A	WFMU	TO	
66067	E	A	WFMU	TO	
66068	E	A	WFMU	TO	
66069	E	A	WFMU	TO	
66070	E	A	WFMU	TO	
66071 *	E	A	WBES	TO	
66072 *	E	A	WBEN	TO	
66074	E	A	WFMU	TO	
66075	E	A	WFMU	TO	
66076	E	A	WFMU	TO	
66077	E	A	WFMU	TO	Benjamin Gimbert G.C.
66078	E	A	WFMU	TO	
66079	E	A	WFMU	TO	James Nightall G.C.
66080	E	A	WFMU	TO	
66081	E	A	WFMU	TO	
66082	E	A	WNWX	LT (S)	
66083	E	A	WFMU	TO	
66084	E	A	WFMU	TO	
66085	E	A	WFMU	TO	
66086	E	A	WFMU	TO	
66087	E	A	WFMU	TO	
66088	E	A	WFMU	TO	
66089	E	A	WFMU	TO	
66090	E	A	WFMU	TO	
66091	E	A	WFMU	TO	
66092	E	A	WFMU	TO	
66093	E	A	WFMU	TO	
66094	E	A	WFMU	TO	

66095	E	A	WFMU	TO
66096	E	A	WFMU	TO
66097	DB	A	WFMU	TO
66098	E	A	WFMU	TO
66099 r	E	A	WFMU	TO
66100 r	E	A	WFMU	TO
66101 r	DB	A	WFMU	TO
66102 r	E	A	WFMU	TO
66103 r	E	A	WFMU	TO
66104 r	E	A	WFMU	TO
66105 r	E	A	WFMU	TO
66106 r	E	A	WFMU	TO
66107 r	E	A	WFMU	TO
66108 r	E	A	WFMU	TO
66109	E	A	WFMU	TO
66110 r	E	A	WFMU	TO
66111 r	E	A	WFMU	TO
66112 r	E	A	WFMU	TO
66113 r	E	A	WFMU	TO
66114 r	E	A	WFMU	TO
66115	E	A	WFMU	TO
66116	E	A	WFMU	TO
66117	E	A	WFMU	TO
66118	E	A	WFMU	TO
66119	E	A	WFMU	TO
66120	E	A	WFMU	TO
66121	E	A	WFMU	TO
66122	E	A	WFMU	TO
66123 *	E	A	WBES	TO
66124	E	A	WFMU	TO
66125	E	A	WFMU	TO
66126	E	A	WFMU	TO
66127	E	A	WFMU	TO
66128	E	A	WFMU	TO
66129	E	A	WFMU	TO
66130	E	A	WFMU	TO
66131	E	A	WFMU	TO
66132	E	A	WFMU	TO
66133	E	A	WFMU	TO
66134	E	A	WFMU	TO
66135	E	A	WFMU	TO
66136	E	A	WFMU	TO
66137	E	A	WFMU	TO
66138	E	A	WFMU	TO
66139	E	A	WFMU	TO
66140	E	A	WFMU	TO
66141	E	A	WFMU	TO
66142	E	A	WFMU	TO
66143	E	A	WFMU	TO
66144	E	A	WFMU	TO
66145	E	A	WFMU	TO

66147	E	A	WFMU	TO	
66148	E	A	WFMU	TO	
66149	E	A	WFMU	TO	
66150	E	A	WFMU	TO	
66151	E	A	WFMU	TO	
66152	DB	A	WFMU	TO	Derek Holmes Railway Operator
66154	E	A	WFMU	TO	
66155	E	A	WFMU	TO	
66156	E	A	WFMU	TO	
66158	E	A	WFMU	TO	
66160	E	A	WFMU	TO	
66161	E	A	WFMU	TO	
66162	E	A	WFMU	TO	
66164	E	A	WFMU	TO	
66165	E	A	WFMU	TO	
66167	E	A	WFMU	TO	
66168	E	A	WFMU	TO	
66169	E	A	WFMU	TO	
66170	E	A	WFMU	TO	
66171	E	A	WFMU	TO	
66172	E	A	WFMU	TO	PAUL MELLENEY
66174	E	A	WFMU	TO	
66175	E	A	WFMU	TO	
66176	E	A	WFMU	TO	
66177	E	A	WFMU	TO	
66181	E	A	WFMU	TO	
66182	E	A	WFMU	TO	
66183	E	A	WFMU	TO	
66184	E	A	WFMU	TO	
66185	E	A	WFMU	TO	
66186	E	A	WFMU	TO	
66187	E	A	WFMU	TO	
66188	E	A	WFMU	TO	
66192	E	A	WFMU	TO	
66193	E	A	WFMU	TO	
66194	E	A	WFMU	TO	
66197	E	A	WFMU	TO	
66198	E	A	WFMU	TO	
66199	E	A	WFMU	TO	
66200	E	A	WFMU	TO	RAILWAY HERITAGE COMMITTEE
66201	E	A	WFMU	TO	
66204	E	A	WFMU	TO	
66206	E	A	WFMU	TO	
66207	E	A	WFMU	TO	
66213	E	A	WFMU	TO	
66218 *	E	A	WBES	TO	
66221	E	A	WBES	TO	
66223 *	E	A	WBES	TO	
66230	E	A	WFMU	TO	
66232	E	A	WFMU	TO	
66238	E	A	WFMU	TO	

66245 *	**E**	A	WBES	TO
66249 *	**E**	A	WBES	TO
66250	**E**	A	WFMU	TO

Class 66/3. Former Fastline-operated loco now operated by DRS. Low emission. Details as Class 66/0 except:

Engine: EMD 12N-710G3B-U2 two stroke of 2420 kW (3245 hp) at 904 rpm.
Traction Motors: General Motors D43TRC.
Fuel Capacity: 5150 litres.

66301	**DS**	BN	XHIM	KM
66302	**DS**	BN	XHIM	KM
66303	**DS**	BN	XHIM	KM
66304	**DS**	BN	XHIM	KM
66305	**DS**	BN	XHIM	KM

66412–434. Low emission. Lloyds Banking Group-owned. Details as Class 66/0 except:

Engine: EMD 12N-710G3B-U2 two stroke of 2420 kW (3245 hp) at 904 rpm.
Traction Motors: General Motors D43TRC.
Fuel Capacity: 5150 litres.

Non-standard liveries: 66412 All over black with a red solebar stripe (formerly Malcolm Rail).
66414 Two tone blue & white (formerly Stobart Rail).

Advertising livery: 66434 Malcolm Rail (blue).

66412	**0**	LY	DFEP	LD (S)
66413	**DS**	LY	DFHG	LD
66414	**0**	LY	DFIN	LD
66415	**DS**	LY	DFTZ	LD
66416	**DS**	LY	DFIN	LD
66418	**DS**	LY	DFIN	LD
66419	**DS**	LY	DFTZ	LD
66420	**DS**	LY	DFIN	LD
66421	**DS**	LY	XHIM	KM
66422	**DS**	LY	XHIM	KM
66423	**DS**	LY	XHIM	KM
66424	**DS**	LY	XHIM	KM
66425	**DS**	LY	XHIM	KM
66426	**DS**	LY	XHIM	KM
66427	**DS**	LY	XHIM	KM
66428	**DS**	LY	XHIM	KM
66429	**DS**	LY	XHIM	KM
66430	**DS**	LY	XHIM	KM
66431	**DS**	LY	XHIM	KM
66432	**DS**	LY	XHIM	KM
66433	**DS**	LY	XHIM	KM
66434	**AL**	LY	XHIM	KM

Class 66/5. Freightliner-operated locos. Details as Class 66/0.

Advertising livery: 66522 Shanks Waste (one half of loco Freightliner green and one half Shanks' Waste light green).

66501	FL	P	DFGM	LD	Japan 2001
66502	FL	P	DFGM	LD	Basford Hall Centenary 2001
66503	FL	P	DFGM	LD	The RAILWAY MAGAZINE
66504	FL	P	DFGM	LD	
66505	FL	P	DFGM	LD	
66506	FL	E	DFHH	LD	Crewe Regeneration
66507	FL	E	DFHH	LD	
66508	FL	E	DFRT	LD	
66509	FL	E	DFHH	LD	
66510	FL	E	DFRT	LD	
66511	FL	E	DFRT	LD	
66512	FL	E	DFHH	LD	
66513	FL	E	DFHH	LD	
66514	FL	E	DFRT	LD	
66515	FL	E	DFRT	LD	
66516	FL	E	DFGM	LD	
66517	FL	E	DFGM	LD	
66518	FL	E	DFHH	LD	
66519	FL	E	DFHH	LD	
66520	FL	E	DFRT	LD	
66522	AL	E	DFRT	LD	
66523	FL	E	DFRT	LD	
66524	FL	E	DFHH	LD	
66525	FL	E	DFHH	LD	
66526	FL	P	DFHH	LD	Driver Steve Dunn (George)
66527	FL	P	DFRT	LD	Don Raider
66528	FL	P	DFHH	LD	
66529	FL	P	DFHH	LD	
66530	FL	P	DFHH	LD	
66531	FL	P	DFHH	LD	
66532	FL	P	DFGM	LD	P&O Nedlloyd Atlas
66533	FL	P	DFGM	LD	Hanjin Express/Senator Express
66534	FL	P	DFGM	LD	OOCL Express
66535	FL	P	DFGM	LD	
66536	FL	P	DFGM	LD	
66537	FL	P	DFGM	LD	
66538	FL	E	DFIM	LD	
66539	FL	E	DFIM	LD	
66540	FL	E	DFIM	LD	Ruby
66541	FL	E	DFIM	LD	
66542	FL	E	DFIM	LD	
66543	FL	E	DFIM	LD	
66544	FL	P	DFHG	LD	
66545	FL	P	DFHG	LD	
66546	FL	P	DFHG	LD	
66547	FL	P	DFHG	LD	
66548	FL	P	DFHG	LD	

66549	FL	P	DFHG	LD	
66550	FL	P	DFHG	LD	
66551	FL	P	DFHG	LD	
66552	FL	P	DFHG	LD	Maltby Raider
66553	FL	P	DFHG	LD	
66554	FL	E	DFHG	LD	
66555	FL	E	DFHG	LD	
66556	FL	E	DFIM	LD	
66557	FL	E	DFHG	LD	
66558	FL	E	DFIM	LD	
66559	FL	E	DFHG	LD	
66560	FL	E	DFHG	LD	
66561	FL	E	DFHG	LD	
66562	FL	E	DFIM	LD	
66563	FL	E	DFIM	LD	
66564	FL	E	DFIM	LD	
66565	FL	E	DFIM	LD	
66566	FL	E	DFIM	LD	
66567	FL	E	DFIM	LD	
66568	FL	E	DFIM	LD	
66569	FL	E	DFIM	LD	
66570	FL	E	DFIM	LD	
66571	FL	E	DFIM	LD	
66572	FL	E	DFIM	LD	

Class 66/5. Freightliner-operated low emission locos. Details as Class 66/0 except:

Engine: EMD 12N-710G3B-U2 two stroke of 2420 kW (3245 hp) at 904 rpm.
Traction Motors: General Motors D43TRC.
Fuel Capacity: 5150 litres.

66585	FL	LY	DFHG	LD	The Drax Flyer
66587	FL	LY	DFIN	LD	
66588	FL	LY	DFIN	LD	
66589	FL	LY	DFIN	LD	
66590	FL	LY	DFIN	LD	
66591	FL	LY	DFIN	LD	
66592	FL	LY	DFIN	LD	Johnson Stevens Agencies
66593	FL	LY	DFIN	LD	3MG MERSEY MULTIMODAL GATEWAY
66594	FL	LY	DFIN	LD	NYK Spirit of Kyoto
66595	FL	BN	DFHG	LD	
66596	FL	BN	DFHG	LD	
66597	FL	BN	DFHG	LD	Viridor
66598	FL	BN	DFHG	LD	
66599	FL	BN	DFHG	LD	

Class 66/6. Freightliner-operated locomotives with modified gear ratios.
Details as Class 66/0 except:

Maximum Tractive Effort: 467 kN (105080 lbf).
Continuous Tractive Effort: 296 kN (66630 lbf) at 14.0 mph.
Design Speed: 65 mph.   **Maximum Speed:** 65 mph.

66601	FL	P	DFHH	LD	The Hope Valley

66602	**FL**	P	DFHH	LD	
66603	**FL**	P	DFHH	LD	
66604	**FL**	P	DFHH	LD	
66605	**FL**	P	DFHH	LD	
66606	**FL**	P	DFHH	LD	
66607	**FL**	P	DFHG	LD	
66610	**FL**	P	DFHG	LD	
66613	**FL**	E	DFHG	LD	
66614	**FL**	E	DFHG	LD	
66615	**FL**	E	DFHG	LD	
66616	**FL**	E	DFHG	LD	
66617	**FL**	E	DFHG	LD	
66618	**FL**	E	DFHG	LD	Railways Illustrated Annual Photographic Awards Alan Barnes Derek W. Johnson MBE
66619	**FL**	E	DFHG	LD	
66620	**FL**	E	DFHG	LD	
66621	**FL**	E	DFHG	LD	
66622	**FL**	E	DFHG	LD	

Class 66/6. Freightliner-operated low emission loco with modified gear ratios.
Fuel Capacity: 5150 litres.

Advertising livery: 66623 Bardon Aggregates (blue).

66623	**AL**	LY	DFHG	LD	Bill Bolsover

Class 66/7. GB Railfreight-operated locos. Details as Class 66/0.

Non-standard/Advertising liveries:

66705 **GB** livery but with the addition of "Union Jack" bodyside vinyls.
66709 MSC – blue with images of a container ship.
66720 Day and night (various colours, different on each side).

66701	**GB**	E	GBCM	PG	
66702	**GB**	E	GBCM	PG	Blue Lightning
66703	**GB**	E	GBCM	PG	Doncaster PSB 1981–2002
66704	**GB**	E	GBCM	PG	Colchester Power Signalbox
66705	**GB**	E	GBCM	PG	Golden Jubilee
66706	**GB**	E	GBCM	PG	Nene Valley
66707	**GB**	E	GBCM	PG	Sir Sam Fay GREAT CENTRAL RAILWAY
66708	**GB**	E	GBCM	PG	Jayne
66709	**AL**	E	GBCM	PG	Sorrento
66710	**GB**	E	GBCM	PG	Phil Packer BRIT
66711	**GB**	E	GBCM	PG	
66712	**GB**	E	GBCM	PG	Peterborough Power Signalbox
66713	**GB**	E	GBCM	PG	Forest City
66714	**GB**	E	GBCM	PG	Cromer Lifeboat
66715	**GB**	E	GBCM	PG	VALOUR – IN MEMORY OF ALL RAILWAY EMPLOYEES WHO GAVE THEIR LIVES FOR THEIR COUNTRY
66716	**GB**	E	GBCM	PG	LOCOMOTIVE & CARRIAGE INSTITUTION CENTENARY 1911–2011
66717	**GB**	E	GBCM	PG	Good Old Boy

66718–746. Low emission. GB Railfreight locos. 66733–737 renumbered from former DRS locos 66401–405. 66738–741 renumbered from former Freightliner locos 66578–581. 66742–746 renumbered from former DRS/Colas Rail locos 66406–410/841–845.

All details as Class 66/0 except 66718–732 as below:

Engine: EMD 12N-710G3B-U2 two stroke of 2420 kW (3245 hp) at 904 rpm.
Traction Motors: General Motors D43TRC.
Fuel Capacity: 5546 litres (66718–722) or 5150 litres (66723–732).

Note: 66734 derailed in June 2012 and landed in a precarious position above Loch Treig, near Tulloch on the West Highland Line. It is currently stored in this position awaiting recovery or disposal.

66718	**MT**	E	GBCM	PG	Gwyneth Dunwoody
66719	**MT**	E	GBCM	PG	METRO-LAND
66720	**O**	E	GBCM	PG	
66721	**MT**	E	GBCM	PG	Harry Beck
66722	**MT**	E	GBCM	PG	Sir Edward Watkin
66723	**FS**	E	GBSD	PG	Chinook
66724	**FS**	E	GBSD	PG	Drax Power Station
66725	**FS**	E	GBSD	PG	SUNDERLAND
66726	**FS**	E	GBSD	PG	SHEFFIELD WEDNESDAY
66727	**FS**	E	GBSD	PG	Andrew Scott CBE
66728	**GB**	P	GBCM	PG	Institution of Railway Operators
66729	**GB**	P	GBCM	PG	DERBY COUNTY
66730	**GB**	P	GBCM	PG	Whitemoor
66731	**GB**	P	GBCM	PG	interhub GB
66732	**GB**	P	GBCM	PG	GBRf The First Decade 1999–2009 John Smith – MD

66733	(66401)	r	**GB**	P	GBFM	PG
66734	(66402)	r	**GB**	P	GBZZ	Tulloch (S)
66735	(66403)	r	**GB**	P	GBFM	PG
66736	(66404)	r	**GB**	P	GBFM	PG WOLVERHAMPTON WANDERERS
66737	(66405)	r	**GB**	P	GBFM	PG Lesia
66738	(66578)		**FL**	GB	GBCM	PG
66739	(66579)		**FL**	GB	GBCM	PG
66740	(66580)		**FL**	GB	GBCM	PG
66741	(66581)		**FL**	GB	GBCM	PG

66742	(66406, 66841)	**GB**	GB	GBRT	PG	ABP Port of Immingham Centenary 1912–2012
66743	(66407, 66842)	**GB**	GB	GBRT	PG	
66744	(66408, 66843)	**GB**	GB	GBRT	PG	Crossrail
66745	(66409, 66844)	**GB**	GB	GBRT	PG	Modern Railways The First 50 Years
66746	(66410, 66845)	**GB**	GB	GBRT	PG	

Class 66/8. Colas Rail locos. Renumbered from former Freightliner locos 66573–577. Details as Class 66/0.

66846	(66573)	**CS**	CS	COLO	RU
66847	(66574)	**CS**	CS	COLO	RU

66848 (66575)	**CS**	CS	COLO	RU	
66849 (66576)	**CS**	CS	COLO	RU	Wylam Dilly
66850 (66577)	**CS**	CS	COLO	RU	

Class 66/9. Freightliner locos. Low emission "demonstrator" locos. Details as Class 66/0 except:

Engine: EMD 12N-710G3B-U2 two stroke of 2420 kW (3245 hp) at 904 rpm.
Traction Motors: General Motors D43TRC.
Fuel Capacity: 5905/5150 litres.

66951	**FL**	E	DFHG	LD
66952	**FL**	E	DFHG	LD

Class 66/9. Freightliner-operated low emission locos. Owing to the 665xx number range being full further orders of 66/5s are to be numbered from 66953 onwards. Details as Class 66/5 (low emission).

66953	**FL**	BN	DFHG	LD	
66954	**FL**	BN	DFIN	LD	
66955	**FL**	BN	DFIN	LD	
66956	**FL**	BN	DFIN	LD	
66957	**FL**	BN	DFHG	LD	Stephenson Locomotive Society 1909–2009

CLASS 67   ALSTOM/GENERAL MOTORS EMD Bo-Bo

Built: 1999–2000 by Alstom at Valencia, Spain, as sub-contractors for General Motors (General Motors model JT42 HW-HS).
Engine: GM 12N-710G3B-EC two stroke of 2385 kW (3200 hp) at 904 rpm.
Main Alternator: General Motors AR9A/HEP7/CA6C.
Traction Motors: General Motors D43FM.
Maximum Tractive Effort: 141 kN (31770 lbf).
Continuous Tractive Effort: 90 kN (20200 lbf) at 46.5 mph.
Power At Rail: 1860 kW.   **Train Brakes:** Air.
Brake Force: 78 t.   **Dimensions:** 19.74 x 2.72 m.
Weight: 90 t.   **Wheel Diameter:** 965 mm.
Design Speed: 125 mph.   **Maximum Speed:** 125 mph.
Fuel Capacity: 4927 litres.   **RA:** 8.
Train Supply: Electric, index 66.   **Multiple Working:** AAR System.

Notes: All equipped with Slow Speed Control and Swinghead Automatic "Buckeye" Combination Couplers.

67004, 67007, 67009 and 67011 are fitted with cast iron brake blocks for working the Fort William Sleeper. **Maximum Speed:** 80 mph.

67004 and 67027 carry their names on one side only.

Non-standard liveries: 67026 Diamond Jubilee silver.

67029 All over silver with DB logos.

67001	**AB**	A	WATN	CE
67002	**AB**	A	WATN	CE
67003	**AB**	A	WATN	CE

67004 r	**E**	A	WABN	CE	Post Haste
67005	**RZ**	A	WATN	CE	Queen's Messenger
67006	**RZ**	A	WAAN	CE	Royal Sovereign
67007 r	**E**	A	WABN	CE	
67008	**E**	A	WAAN	CE	
67009 r	**E**	A	WABN	CE	
67010	**WS**	A	WAWN	CE	
67011 r	**E**	A	WNWX	TO (S)	
67012	**WS**	A	WAWN	CE	A Shropshire Lad
67013	**WS**	A	WAWN	CE	Dyfrbont Pontcysyllte
67014	**WS**	A	WAWN	CE	Thomas Telford
67015	**WS**	A	WAWN	CE	David J. Lloyd
67016	**E**	A	WAAN	CE	
67017	**E**	A	WAAN	CE	Arrow
67018	**DB**	A	WAWN	CE	Keith Heller
67019	**E**	A	WAAN	CE	
67020	**E**	A	WAAN	CE	
67021	**E**	A	WAAN	CE	
67022	**E**	A	WAAN	CE	
67023	**E**	A	WAAN	CE	
67024	**E**	A	WAAN	CE	
67025	**E**	A	WAAN	CE	Western Star
67026	**0**	A	WAAN	CE	Diamond Jubilee
67027	**E**	A	WAAN	CE	Rising Star
67028	**E**	A	WAAN	CE	
67029	**0**	A	WAAN	CE	Royal Diamond
67030 r	**E**	A	WABN	CE	

CLASS 68   VOSSLOH   Bo-Bo

New Vossloh "UKLight" locos on order for DRS, due for delivery 2013–14. Full
details awaited.

Built: 2012–13 by Vossloh, Valencia, Spain.
Engine: Caterpillar C175-16 of 2800 kW at 3750 hp at 1740 rpm.
Main Alternator:
Traction Motors:
Maximum Tractive Effort: 317 kN (71 260 lbf).
Continuous Tractive Effort:

Power At Rail:	**Train Brakes:** Air.
Brake Force:	**Dimensions:**
Weight: 85 t.	**Wheel Diameter:**
Design Speed: 100 mph.	**Maximum Speed:** 100 mph.
Fuel Capacity: 5000 litres.	**RA:**
Train Supply:	**Multiple Working:**

68001
68002
68003
68004
68005
68006

68007
68008
68009
68010
68011
68012
68013
68014
68015

CLASS 70   GENERAL ELECTRIC   Co-Co

New GE "PowerHaul" Freightliner locos. An option exists for a further ten locos. 70012 was badly damaged whilst being unloaded in 2011 and was returned to Pennsylvania. 70099 is a Turkish-built Class 70 demonstrator that was due to arrive in Britain in late 2012.

Built: 2009–11 by General Electric, Erie, Pennsylvania, USA.
Engine: General Electric PowerHaul P616LDA1 of 2848 kW (3820 hp) at 1500 rpm.
Main Alternator: General Electric GTA series.
Traction Motors: AC-GE 5GEB30.
Maximum Tractive Effort: 544 kN (122 000 lbf).
Continuous Tractive Effort: 427 kN (96 000 lbf) at ?? m.p.h.
Power At Rail: **Train Brakes:** Air.
Brake Force: 96.7 t.   **Dimensions:** 21.71 x 2.64 m.
Weight: 129 t.   **Wheel Diameter:** 1066 mm.
Design Speed: 75 mph.   **Maximum Speed:** 75 mph.
Fuel Capacity: 6000 litres.   **RA:** 7.
Train Supply: Not equipped.   **Multiple Working:** AAR System.

70001	**FH**	LY	DFGI	LD	PowerHaul
70002	**FH**	LY	DFGH	LD	
70003	**FH**	LY	DFGH	LD	
70004	**FH**	LY	DFGH	LD	The Coal Industry Society
70005	**FH**	LY	DFGH	LD	
70006	**FH**	LY	DFGH	LD	
70007	**FH**	LY	DFGI	LD	
70008	**FH**	LY	DFGI	LD	
70009	**FH**	LY	DFGI	LD	
70010	**FH**	LY	DFGH	LD	
70011	**FH**	LY	DFGH	LD	
70013	**FH**	LY	DFGH	LD	
70014	**FH**	LY	DFGH	LD	
70015	**FH**	LY	DFGH	LD	
70016	**FH**	LY	DFGH	LD	
70017	**FH**	LY	DFGI	LD	
70018	**FH**	LY	DFGI	LD	
70019	**FH**	LY	DFGI	LD	
70020	**FH**	LY	DFGI	LD	

70099

2. ELECTRO-DIESEL & ELECTRIC LOCOMOTIVES

CLASS 73   BR/ENGLISH ELECTRIC   Bo-Bo

Electro-diesel locomotives which can operate either from a DC supply or using power from a diesel engine.

Built: 1965–67 by English Electric Co. at Vulcan Foundry, Newton-le-Willows.
Engine: English Electric 4SRKT of 447 kW (600 hp) at 850 rpm.
Main Generator: English Electric 824/5D.
Electric Supply System: 750 V DC from third rail.
Traction Motors: English Electric 546/1B.
Maximum Tractive Effort (Electric): 179 kN (40000 lbf).
Maximum Tractive Effort (Diesel): 160 kN (36000 lbf).
Continuous Rating (Electric): 1060 kW (1420 hp) giving a tractive effort of 35 kN (7800 lbf) at 68 mph.
Continuous Tractive Effort (Diesel): 60 kN (13600 lbf) at 11.5 mph.
Maximum Rail Power (Electric): 2350 kW (3150 hp) at 42 mph.
Train Brakes: Air, vacuum & electro-pneumatic († Air & electro-pneumatic).
Brake Force: 31 t.   **Dimensions:** 16.36 x 2.64 m.
Weight: 77 t.   **Wheel Diameter:** 1016 mm.
Design Speed: 90 mph.   **Maximum Speed:** 90 mph.
Fuel Capacity: 1409 litres.   **RA:** 6.
Train Supply: Electric, index 66 (on electric power only).
Multiple Working: SR 27-way System & Blue Star.

Formerly numbered E6001–E6020/E6022–E6026/E6028–E6049 (not in order).

Note: Locomotives numbered in the 732xx series are classed as 73/2 and were originally dedicated to Gatwick Express services.

Non-standard liveries: 73107 Two-tone grey.
73139 Weardale Railway Brown & cream.

73101	**PC**	RE	RVLO	ZA (S)
73104	**IC**	RE	RVLO	ZA (S)
73107	**O**	20	MBED	SE	Redhill 1844–1994
73109	**SD**	TT	MBED	SL	Battle of Britain 50th Anniversary
73119	**B**	GB	GBED	SE	Borough of Eastleigh
73133	**TT**	TT	MBED	SU	
73136	**TT**	TT	MBED	SU	Perseverance
73138	**Y**	NR	QADD	ZA	
73139	**O**	RE	RVLO	ZA (S)	
73141	**FS**	GB	GBED	SE	Charlotte
73201 †	**B**	20	MBED	SE	Broadlands
73202 †	**GV**	P	MBED	SL	Dave Berry
73204 †	**GB**	GB	GBED	SE	Janice
73205 †	**IC**	GB	GBED	SE	Jeanette
73206 †	**GB**	GB	GBED	SE	Lisa

73207 †	**BL**	GB	GBED	SE	
73208 †	**B**	GB	GBED	SE	Kirsten
73209 †	**GB**	GB	GBZZ	LB (S)	Alison
73211 †	**GX**	RE	RVLO	ZA (S)	
73212 †	**FS**	GB	GBED	SE	
73213 †	**FS**	GB	GBED	SE	
73235 †	**SD**	P	HYWD	WD	

CLASS 86   BR/ENGLISH ELECTRIC   Bo-Bo

Built: 1965–66 by English Electric Co at Vulcan Foundry, Newton-le-Willows or by BR at Doncaster Works.
Electric Supply System: 25 kV AC 50 Hz overhead.
Train Brakes: Air.   **Brake Force:** 40 t.
Dimensions: 17.83 x 2.65 m.   **Weight:** 83–86.8 t.
RA: 6.   **Multiple Working:** TDM system.
Train Supply: Electric, index 66.

Formerly numbered E3101–E3200 (not in order).

Class 86/1. Class 87-type bogies & motors.

Details as above except:
Traction Motors: GEC 412AZ frame mounted.
Maximum Tractive Effort: 258 kN (58000 lbf).
Continuous Rating: 3730 kW (5000 hp) giving a tractive effort of 95 kN (21300 lbf) at 87 mph.
Maximum Rail Power: 5860 kW (7860 hp) at 50.8 mph.
Wheel Diameter: 1150 mm.   **Weight:** 86.8 t.
Design Speed: 110 m.p.h.   **Maximum Speed:** 110 mph.

86101	**B**	EL	ACAC	WN	Sir William A Stanier FRS

Class 86/2. Standard design rebuilt with resilient wheels & Flexicoil suspension.

Traction Motors: AEI 282BZ axle hung.
Maximum Tractive Effort: 207 kN (46500 lbf).
Continuous Rating: 3010 kW (4040 hp) giving a tractive effort of 85 kN (19200 lbf) at 77.5 mph.
Maximum Rail Power: 4550 kW (6100 hp.) at 49.5 mph.
Wheel Diameter: 1156 mm.   **Weight:** 85–86.2 t.
Design Speed: 125 mph.   **Maximum Speed:** 100 mph.

Non-standard livery/numbering: 86233 & 86259 BR "Electric blue" livery. 86233 Also carries number E3172.

86213	**IC**	EL	ACXX	WB (S)	Lancashire Witch
86228	**IC**	EP	EPXS	LM (S)	
86229	**V**	EP	EPXX	LM (S)	
86231	**V**	EP	EPXS	LM (S)	
86233	**0**	EP	EPXX	LM (S)	
86234	**AR**	EP	EPXS	LM (S)	
86235	**AR**	EP	EPXS	LM (S)	

86242	AR	EP	EPXX	LM (S)
86246	AR	EP	EPXS	LM (S)
86247	EX	X	DHLT	CP (S)
86251	V	EP	EPXX	LM (S)
86259	O	PP	MBEL	WN	Les Ross

Class 86/4.

Traction Motors: AEI 282AZ axle hung.
Maximum Tractive Effort: 258 kN (58000 lbf).
Continuous Rating: 2680 kW (3600 hp) giving a tractive effort of 89 kN (20000 lbf) at 67 mph.
Maximum Rail Power: 4400 kW (5900 hp) at 38 mph.
Wheel Diameter: 1156 mm. **Weight:** 83–83.9 t.
Design Speed: 100 mph. **Maximum Speed:** 100 mph.

| 86401 | N | EL | ACXX | WN (S) Northampton Town |
| 86424 | Y | EL | ACXX | LM (S) |

Class 86/5. Regeared locomotive operated by Freightliner.

Details as Class 86/4 except:

Continuous Rating: 2680 kW (3600 hp) giving a tractive effort of 117 kN (26300 lbf) at 67 mph.
Maximum Speed: 75 mph. **Train Supply:** Electric, isolated.

| 86501 (86608) | FL | FL | DFGC | CP |

Class 86/6. Freightliner-operated locomotives.

Details as Class 86/4 except:

Maximum Speed: 75 mph. **Train Supply:** Electric, isolated.

86604	FL	FL	DFNC	CP
86605	FL	FL	DFNC	CP
86607	FL	FL	DFNC	CP
86609	FL	FL	DFNC	CP
86610	FL	FL	DFNC	CP
86612	FL	P	DFNC	CP
86613	FL	P	DFNC	CP
86614	FL	P	DFNC	CP
86621	FL	EP	EPXX	CP (S)
86622	FH	P	DFNC	CP
86627	FL	P	DFNC	CP
86628	FL	P	DFNC	CP
86632	FL	P	DFNC	CP
86633	FF	EP	EPXX	CP (S)
86635	FL	EP	EPXX	CP (S)
86637	FH	P	DFNC	CP
86638	FL	P	DFNC	CP
86639	FL	P	DFNC	CP

Class 86/7. Europhoenix-owned locomotives. Refurbished Class 86/2s for the UK spot-hire market. Details as Class 86/2 unless stated.

Maximum Speed: 110 mph. **Weight:** 85t.
Train Supply: Electric, index 74.

86701	(86205)	**CS** EP	COLO	WN	Orion
86702	(86260)	**EL** EP	ETLO	WN	Cassiopeia

Class 86/9. Network Rail-owned locomotives. Rebuilt from Class 86/2s for use as Mobile Load Bank test locos to test Overhead Line Equipment, initially on the WCML. No. 1 end Traction Motors isolated. Can still move under own power.

Maximum Speed: 60 mph. **Train Supply:** Electric, isolated.

86901	(86253)	**Y** NR	QACL	CP	CHIEF ENGINEER
86902	(86210)	**Y** NR	QACL	CP	RAIL VEHICLE ENGINEERING

CLASS 87 BREL/GEC Bo-Bo

Built: 1973–75 by BREL at Crewe Works.
Electric Supply System: 25 kV AC 50 Hz overhead.
Traction Motors: GEC G412AZ frame mounted.
Maximum Tractive Effort: 258 kN (58000 lbf).
Continuous Rating: 3730 kW (5000 hp) giving a tractive effort of 95 kN (21300 lbf) at 87 mph.
Maximum Rail Power: 5860 kW (7860 hp) at 50.8 mph.
Train Brakes: Air. **Brake Force:** 40 t.
Dimensions: 17.83 x 2.65 m. **Weight:** 83.3 t.
Wheel Diameter: 1150 mm. **Design Speed:** 110 mph.
Maximum Speed: 110 mph. **Train Supply:** Electric, index 95.
RA: 6. **Multiple Working:** TDM system.

87002	**B**	EL	ACAC	WN	Royal Sovereign
87009	**V**	EP	EPXS	LM (S)	
87025	**V**	X	SBXL	LM (S)	

CLASS 90 GEC Bo-Bo

Built: 1987–90 by BREL at Crewe Works (as sub contractors for GEC).
Electric Supply System: 25 kV AC 50 Hz overhead.
Traction Motors: GEC G412CY frame mounted.
Maximum Tractive Effort: 258 kN (58000 lbf).
Continuous Rating: 3730 kW (5000 hp) giving a tractive effort of 95 kN (21300 lbf) at 87 mph.
Maximum Rail Power: 5860 kW (7860 hp) at 68.3 mph.
Train Brakes: Air.
Brake Force: 40 t. **Dimensions:** 18.80 x 2.74 m.
Weight: 84.5 t. **Wheel Diameter:** 1150 mm.
Design Speed: 110 mph. **Maximum Speed:** 110 mph.
Train Supply: Electric, index 95. **RA:** 7.
Multiple Working: TDM system.

Non-standard livery: 90036 As **FE** but with a yellow roof. EWS stickers.

90001 b	1	P	IANA	NC		
90002 b	1	P	IANA	NC		
90003 b	NX	P	IANA	NC		Rædwald of East Anglia
90004 b	1	P	IANA	NC		Eastern Daily Press 1870–2010
						SERVING NORFOLK FOR 140 YEARS
90005 b	1	P	IANA	NC		Vice-Admiral Lord Nelson
90006 b	1	P	IANA	NC		Modern Railways Magazine/
						Roger Ford
90007 b	1	P	IANA	NC		Sir John Betjeman
90008 b	NX	P	IANA	NC		The East Anglian
90009 b	1	P	IANA	NC		Diamond Jubilee
90010 b	1	P	IANA	NC		BRESSINGHAM STEAM & GARDENS
90011 b	1	P	IANA	NC		Let's Go East of England
90012 b	1	P	IANA	NC		Royal Anglian Regiment
90013 b	1	P	IANA	NC		The Evening Star
						PRIDE OF IPSWICH 1885–2010
						125 YEARS OF SERVING SUFFOLK
90014 b	1	P	IANA	NC		Norfolk and Norwich Festival
90015 b	NX	P	IANA	NC		Colchester Castle
90016	FL	P	DFLC	CP		
90017 b	E	DB	WNTS	CE	(S)	
90018 b	E	DB	WEFE	CE		
90019 b	FS	DB	WEFE	CE		
90020 b	E	DB	WEFE	CE		Collingwood
90021	FS	DB	WNTR	CE		
90022	EG	DB	WNTS	CE	(S)	Freightconnection
90023	E	DB	WNTS	CE	(S)	
90024	FS	DB	WEFE	CE		
90025	F	DB	WNTS	CE	(S)	
90026	E	DB	WEFE	CE		
90027	F	DB	WNTS	CE	(S)	Allerton T&RS Depot
90028	E	DB	WEFE	CE		
90029	E	DB	WEFE	CE		The Institution of Civil Engineers
90030	E	DB	WNTS	CE	(S)	Crewe Locomotive Works
90031	E	DB	WNTS	CE	(S)	The Railway Children Partnership
						Working For Street Children Worldwide
90032	E	DB	WNTS	CE	(S)	
90033	FE	DB	WNTS	CE	(S)	
90034	E	DB	WNTS	CE	(S)	
90035	E	DB	WEFE	CE		
90036	0	DB	WNTR	CE		
90037	E	DB	WNTS	CE	(S)	Spirit of Dagenham
90038	FE	DB	WNTS	CE	(S)	
90039	E	DB	WEFE	CE		
90040	E	DB	WNTS	CE	(S)	The Railway Mission
90041	FL	P	DFLC	CP		
90042	FF	P	DFLC	CP	(S)	
90043	FF	P	DFLC	CP		Freightliner Coatbridge
90044	FF	P	DFLC	CP		

90045	**FH**	P	DFLC	CP
90046	**FL**	P	DFLC	CP
90047	**FF**	P	DFLC	CP
90048	**FF**	P	DFLC	CP
90049	**FH**	P	DFLC	CP
90050	**FF**	AV	MBEL	CP (S)

CLASS 91   GEC   Bo-Bo

Built: 1988–91 by BREL at Crewe Works (as sub contractors for GEC).
Electric Supply System: 25 kV AC 50 Hz overhead.
Traction Motors: GEC G426AZ.
Maximum Tractive Effort: 190 kN (43 000 lbf).
Continuous Rating: 4540 kW (6090 hp) giving a tractive effort of 170kN at 96mph.
Maximum Rail Power: 4700 kW (6300 hp) at ?? mph.
Train Brakes: Air.
Brake Force: 45 t.
Weight: 84 t.
Design Speed: 140 mph.
Train Supply: Electric, index 95.
Multiple Working: TDM system.

Dimensions: 19.41 x 2.74 m.
Wheel Diameter: 1000 mm.
Maximum Speed: 125 mph.
RA: 7.

Note: Locos originally numbered in the 910xx series, but renumbered upon completion of overhauls at Bombardier, Doncaster by the addition of 100 to their original number. The exception to this rule was 91023 which was renumbered 91132.

Advertising liveries: 91101 Flying Scotsman (purple).

91110 Battle of Britain (black and grey).

91101	**AL**	E	IECA	BN	
91102	**EC**	E	IECA	BN	City of York
91103	**EC**	E	IECA	BN	
91104	**EC**	E	IECA	BN	
91105	**EC**	E	IECA	BN	
91106	**EC**	E	IECA	BN	
91107	**EC**	E	IECA	BN	
91108	**EC**	E	IECA	BN	
91109	**EC**	E	IECA	BN	Sir Bobby Robson
91110	**AL**	E	IECA	BN	BATTLE OF BRITAIN MEMORIAL FLIGHT
91111	**NX**	E	IECA	BN	
91112	**EC**	E	IECA	BN	
91113	**GN**	E	IECA	BN	
91114	**GN**	E	IECA	BN	
91115	**EC**	E	IECA	BN	Blaydon Races
91116	**EC**	E	IECA	BN	
91117	**EC**	E	IECA	BN	WEST RIDING LIMITED
91118	**GN**	E	IECA	BN	
91119	**GN**	E	IECA	BN	
91120	**EC**	E	IECA	BN	

91121	**GN**	E	IECA	BN
91122	**EC**	E	IECA	BN
91124	**GN**	E	IECA	BN
91125	**GN**	E	IECA	BN
91126	**EC**	E	IECA	BN
91127	**EC**	E	IECA	BN
91128	**EC**	E	IECA	BN
91129	**EC**	E	IECA	BN
91130	**EC**	E	IECA	BN
91131	**EC**	E	IECA	BN
91132	**EC**	E	IECA	BN

CLASS 92   BRUSH   Co-Co

Built: 1993–96 by Brush Traction at Loughborough.
Electric Supply System: 25 kV AC 50 Hz overhead or 750 V DC third rail.
Traction Motors: Asea Brown Boveri design. Model 6FRA 7059B (Asynchronous 3-phase induction motors).
Maximum Tractive Effort: 400 kN (90 000 lbf).
Continuous Rating: 5040 kW (6760 hp) on AC, 4000 kW (5360 hp) on DC.
Maximum Rail Power: **Train Brakes:** Air.
Brake Force: 63 t.   **Dimensions:** 21.34 x 2.67 m.
Weight: 126 t.   **Wheel Diameter:** 1070 mm.
Design Speed: 140 km/h (87 mph).   **Maximum Speed:** 145 km/h (90 mph).
Train Supply: Electric, index 108 (AC), 70 (DC).
RA: 7.

Advertising livery: 92017 Stobart Rail (two tone blue & white).

92001	**E**	LY	WNTR	CE (S)	Victor Hugo
92002	**EG**	LY	WNWX	CE (S)	H.G. Wells
92003	**EG**	LY	WTAE	CE	Beethoven
92004	**EG**	LY	WNWX	CE (S)	Jane Austen
92005	**EG**	LY	WNTR	CE (S)	Mozart
92006	**EP**	ET	PTXX	CO (S)	Louis Armand
92007	**EG**	LY	WNTR	CE (S)	Schubert
92008	**EG**	LY	WNWX	CE (S)	Jules Verne
92009	**DB**	LY	WNTR	CE (S)	Marco Polo
92010	**EP**	ET	PTXX	CO	Molière
92011	**EG**	LY	WTAE	CE	Handel
92012	**EG**	LY	WNTR	CE (S)	Thomas Hardy
92013	**EG**	LY	WNWX	CE (S)	Puccini
92014	**EP**	ET	PTXX	CO (S)	Emile Zola
92015	**DB**	LY	WTHE	CE	
92016	**DB**	LY	WTHE	CE	
92017	**AL**	LY	WNTR	CE (S)	Bart the Engine
92018	**EP**	ET	PTXX	CO (S)	Stendhal
92019	**EG**	LY	WTAE	CE	Wagner
92020	**EP**	ET	PTXX	CO (S)	Milton
92021	**EP**	ET	PTXX	CO (S)	Purcell
92022	**EG**	LY	WNTR	CE (S)	Charles Dickens
92023	**EP**	ET	PTXX	CO (S)	Ravel

92024	**EG**	LY	WNWX	CE (S)	J.S. Bach
92025	**EG**	LY	WTAE	CE	Oscar Wilde
92026	**EG**	LY	WNTR	CE (S)	Britten
92027	**EG**	LY	WNTR	CE (S)	George Eliot
92028	**EP**	ET	GBET	CO	Saint Saëns
92029	**EG**	LY	WNWX	CE (S)	Dante
92030	**EG**	LY	WTAE	CE	Ashford
92031	**DB**	LY	WTHE	CE	
92032	**GB**	ET	GBET	CO	IMechE Railway Division
92033	**EP**	ET	PTXX	CO (S)	Berlioz
92035	**EP**	LY	WNWX	CE (S)	Mendelssohn
92036	**EG**	LY	WTHE	CE	Bertolt Brecht
92037	**EG**	LY	WTAE	CE	Sullivan
92038	**EP**	ET	GBET	CO	Voltaire
92039	**EG**	LY	WNWX	CE (S)	Johann Strauss
92040	**EP**	ET	PTXX	CO (S)	Goethe
92041	**EG**	LY	WTAE	CE	Vaughan Williams
92042	**DB**	LY	WTHE	CE	
92043	**EP**	ET	GBET	CO	Debussy
92044	**EP**	ET	GBET	CO	Couperin
92045	**EP**	ET	PTXX	LB (S)	Chaucer
92046	**EP**	ET	PTXX	LB (S)	Sweelinck

3. EUROTUNNEL LOCOMOTIVES

DIESEL LOCOMOTIVES

0001–0007   MaK   Bo-Bo

Built: 1991–92 by MaK at Kiel, Germany (Model DE1004).
Engine: MTU 12V 396 TC13 of 940 kW (1260 hp) at 1800 rpm.
Main Alternator: ABB.   **Traction Motors:** ABB.
Maximum Tractive Effort: 305 kN (68600 lbf).
Continuous Tractive Effort: 140 kN (31500 lbf) at 20 mph.
Power At Rail: 750 kW (1012 hp).   **Dimensions:** 14.40 x ?? m.
Brake Force: 120 kN.   **Wheel Diameter:** 1000 mm.
Weight: 82 t.   **Maximum Speed:** 100 km/h.
Design Speed: 120 km/h.   **Train Brakes:** Air.
Fuel Capacity: 3500 litres.   **Multiple Working:** Within class.
Train Supply: Not equipped.   **Signalling System:** TVM430 cab signalling.

Note: Registered on TOPS as 21901–907.

0001	**GY**	ET	CO
0002	**GY**	ET	CO
0003	**GY**	ET	CO
0004	**GY**	ET	CO
0005	**GY**	ET	CO

The following two locos were rebuilt from NS 6400 Class 6456 and 6457 (built 1991) and added to the Eurotunnel fleet in 2011.

0006	**GY**	ET	CO
0007	**GY**	ET	CO

0031–0042   HUNSLET/SCHÖMA   0-4-0

Built: 1989–90 by Hunslet Engine Company at Leeds as 900 mm gauge.
Rebuilt: 1993–94 by Schöma in Germany to 1435 mm. gauge.
Engine: Deutz of 270 kW (200 hp) at ???? rpm.
Transmission: Mechanical.   **Maximum Tractive Effort:**
Cont. Tractive Effort: **Power At Rail:**
Brake Force: **Dimensions:**
Weight: **Wheel Diameter:**
Design Speed: 50 km/h.   **Maximum Speed:** 50 km/h.
Fuel Capacity: **Train Brakes:** Air.
Train Supply: Not equipped.   **Multiple Working:** Not equipped.

Note: * Rebuilt with inspection platforms to check overhead catenary.

0031	**GY**	ET	CO	FRANCES
0032	**GY**	ET	CO	ELISABETH
0033	**GY**	ET	CO	SILKE

0034		**GY**	ET	CO	AMANDA
0035		**GY**	ET	CO	MARY
0036		**GY**	ET	CO	LAURENCE
0037		**GY**	ET	CO	LYDIE
0038		**GY**	ET	CO	JENNY
0039	*	**GY**	ET	CO	PACITA
0040		**GY**	ET	CO	JILL
0041	*	**GY**	ET	CO	KIM
0042		**GY**	ET	CO	NICOLE

ELECTRIC LOCOMOTIVES

9005–9840   BRUSH/ABB   Bo-Bo-Bo

Built: 1993–2002 by Brush Traction at Loughborough.
Supply System: 25 kV AC 50 Hz overhead.
Traction Motors: Asea Brown Boveri design. Asynchronous 3-phase motors.
Model 6FHA 7059 (as built). Model 6FHA 7059C (7000 kW rated locos).
Maximum Tractive Effort: 400kN (90 000 lbf).
Continuous Rating: Class 9/0 and 9/1: 5760 kW (7725 hp). Class 9/7 and 9/8:
7000 kW (9387 hp).

Maximum Rail Power:	**Multiple Working:** TDM system.
Brake Force: 50 t.	**Dimensions:** 22.01 x 2.97 x 4.20 m.
Weight: 136 t.	**Wheel Diameter:** 1250 mm.
Design Speed: 100 mph.	**Maximum Speed:** 100 mph.
Train Supply: Electric.	**Train Brakes:** Air.

Class 9/0 Original build locos. Built 1993–94.

9005	**EB**	ET	CO	JESSYE NORMAN
9007	**EB**	ET	CO	DAME JOAN SUTHERLAND
9011	**EB**	ET	CO	JOSÉ VAN DAM
9013	**EB**	ET	CO	MARIA CALLAS
9015	**EB**	ET	CO	LÖTSCHBERG 1913
9018	**EB**	ET	CO	WILHELMENIA FERNANDEZ
9022	**EB**	ET	CO	DAME JANET BAKER
9024	**EB**	ET	CO	GOTTHARD 1882
9026	**EB**	ET	CO	FURKATUNNEL 1982
9029	**EB**	ET	CO	THOMAS ALLEN
9033	**EB**	ET	CO	MONTSERRAT CABALLE
9036	**EB**	ET	CO	ALAIN FONDARY
9037	**EB**	ET	CO	GABRIEL BACQUIER

Class 9/7. Increased power freight shuttle locos. Built 2001–02 (9711–23
built 1998–2001 as 9101–13 and rebuilt as 9711–23 2010–12).

9701	**EB**	ET	CO
9702	**EB**	ET	CO
9703	**EB**	ET	CO
9704	**EB**	ET	CO

9705		**EB**	ET	CO
9706		**EB**	ET	CO
9707		**EB**	ET	CO

9711	(9101)	**EB**	ET	CO
9712	(9102)	**EB**	ET	CO
9713	(9103)	**EB**	ET	CO
9714	(9104)	**EB**	ET	CO
9715	(9105)	**EB**	ET	CO
9716	(9106)	**EB**	ET	CO
9717	(9107)	**EB**	ET	CO
9718	(9108)	**EB**	ET	CO
9719	(9109)	**EB**	ET	CO
9720	(9110)	**EB**	ET	CO
9721	(9111)	**EB**	ET	CO
9722	(9112)	**EB**	ET	CO
9723	(9113)	**EB**	ET	CO

Class 9/8 Locos rebuilt from Class 9/0 by adding 800 to the loco number. Uprated to 7000 kW.

9801	**EB**	ET	CO		LESLEY GARRETT
9802	**EB**	ET	CO		STUART BURROWS
9803	**EB**	ET	CO		BENJAMIN LUXON
9804	**EB**	ET	CO		VICTORIA DE LOS ANGELES
9806	**EB**	ET	CO		REGINE CRESPIN
9808	**EB**	ET	CO		ELISABETH SODERSTROM
9809	**EB**	ET	CO		FRANÇOISE POLLET
9810	**EB**	ET	CO		JEAN-PHILIPPE COURTIS
9812	**EB**	ET	CO		LUCIANO PAVAROTTI
9814	**EB**	ET	CO		LUCIA POPP
9816	**EB**	ET	CO		WILLARD WHITE
9817	**EB**	ET	CO	(S)	JOSÉ CARRERAS
9819	**EB**	ET	CO		MARIA EWING
9820	**EB**	ET	CO		NICOLAI GHIAROV
9821	**EB**	ET	CO		TERESA BERGANZA
9823	**EB**	ET	CO		DAME ELISABETH LEGGE-SCHWARZKOPF
9825	**EB**	ET	CO		
9827	**EB**	ET	CO		BARBARA HENDRICKS
9828	**EB**	ET	CO		DAME KIRI TE KANAWA
9831	**EB**	ET	CO		
9832	**EB**	ET	CO		RENATA TEBALDI
9834	**EB**	ET	CO		MIRELLA FRENI
9835	**EB**	ET	CO		NICOLAI GEDDA
9838	**EB**	ET	CO		HILDEGARD BEHRENS
9840	**EB**	ET	CO		

▲ Colas Rail started using its Class 56 fleet on its steel and timber trains in 2012. On 24/07/12 56094 passes Dunkirk, on the outskirts of Nottingham, with 6M08 17.20 Boston Docks–Washwood Heath loaded steel.
Ben Wheeler

▲ DB Schenker-liveried 59201 is seen near Frome with 4C57 14.00 Acton–Merehead Quarry empty stone train on 24/07/12. **Kevin Poole**

▼ Tata steel-liveried 60099 passes Halebank with 6F78 11.30 Fiddlers Ferry–Liverpool Bulk Terminal empty coal on 14/01/12. **Andrew Wills**

▲ Freightliner-liveried 66619 "Derek W. Johnson MBE" passes Upton Scudamore with 6O49 15.00 Theale–Wool on 14/07/11. **Kevin Poole**

▼ DRS 66428 is seen shunting the Tesco intermodal train at Inverness on 03/08/12. **Alexander Colley**

▲ Arriva Trains-liveried 67003 hauls the 16.15 Cardiff Central–Holyhead through Penmaenmawr on 09/08/12. The departure time of this loco-hauled train from Cardiff has since changed to 18.21.

Terry Eyres

Carrying a special silver livery for the Diamond Jubilee, 67026 hauls the
Royal Train empty stock through Baldock en route from Hitchin to Cambridge on
14/06/12.   **Nigel Gibbs**

Freightliner 70017 passes St Denys with a well loaded 4O27 05.40 Garston–
Southampton intermodal on 02/08/12.   **Andrew Mist**

▲ Gatwick Express Thunderbird/standby loco 73202 at Stewarts Lane depot o
26/07/12.   **Brian Dento**

▼ The unique 86501 passes Ardleigh on the Great Eastern Main Line with 4M8
14.36 Felixstowe–Ditton on 03/08/12.   **Antony Gupp**

▲ New Freightliner-liveried 90045 passes Gayton, Northamptonshire with the 14.03 London Euston–Birmingham New Street on 25/05/12. **John Turner**

▼ East Coast grey-liveried 91103 passes Claypole, near Grantham, with the 16.08 London King's Cross–Newark North Gate on 23/05/11. **Lindsay Atkinson**

▲ Two-tone grey-liveried 92019 "Wagner" passes Carnforth with 4S43 Daventry-Mossend Tesco intermodal on 22/08/11. **Tom McAtee**

▼ Eurotunnel MaK locos 0004 and 0005 make for a rare sight at London St Pancras on 21/03/12. **Alisdair Anderson**

4. FORMER BR MAIN LINE LOCOS IN INDUSTRIAL SERVICE

Former British Rail main line locomotives considered to be in "industrial use" are listed here. These locomotives do not currently have Network Rail engineering acceptance for operation on the national railway network.

Number Other no./name   Location

Class 11

12088		Butterwell Disposal Point, Ashington, Northumberland

Class 03

03179	CLIVE	First Capital Connect, Hornsey Depot, London
03196	JOYCE/GLYNIS	West Coast Railway Company, Carnforth
D2381		West Coast Railway Company, Carnforth

Class 07

07001		Barrow Hill Roundhouse, Chesterfield, Derbyshire
D2991	07007	Knights Rail Services, Eastleigh Works, Hampshire
07013		Barrow Hill Roundhouse, Chesterfield, Derbyshire

Class 08

08202	CHUFFER	The Potter Group, Queen Adelaide, Ely
08331		Midland Railway-Butterley, Derbyshire
08375	21	PD Ports, Teesport, Grangetown, Middlesbrough
08389		Nemesis Rail, Burton-upon-Trent, Staffordshire
08393		LH Group, Barton-under-Needwood, Staffordshire
08401		Whitemoor Yard, March, Cambridgeshire
08411		Colne Valley Railway, Halstead, Essex
08417		RVEL, RTC Business Park, Derby
08418		West Coast Railway Company, Carnforth
08423	H011 14	PD Ports, Teesport, Grangetown, Middlesbrough
08441		Felixstowe Dock & Railway Company, Felixstowe
08442	RICHARD J. WENHAM EASTLEIGH DEPOT	LNWR, Eastleigh Depot, Hampshire
08445		Daventry International Railfreight Terminal, Crick
08447		John G Russell (Transport), Hillington, Glasgow
08460		Colne Valley Railway, Halstead, Essex
08484	CAPTAIN NATHANIEL DARELL	Gloucestershire Warwickshire Railway
08485		West Coast Railway Company, Carnforth
08499		Colas Rail, Canton Depot, Cardiff
08502		Barrow Hill Roundhouse, Chesterfield
08503		Railway Support Services, Rye Farm, Wishaw, Sutton Coldfield
08507		Victoria Group, Port of Boston, Boston
08511		Felixstowe Dock & Railway Company, Felixstowe
08516	RORY	LNWR, Barton Hill Depot, Bristol

08523		PD Ports, Teesport, Grangetown, Middlesbrough
08527		Flixborough Wharf, Flixborough, Scunthorpe
08536		RVEL, RTC Business Park, Derby
08568	St. Rollox	Railcare, Springburn Depot, Glasgow
08573		Bombardier Transportation, Ilford Works, London
08588	17	Hanson Traction/Cemex UK, Washwood Heath, Birmingham
08598	H016 HERCULES	The Potter Group, Queen Adelaide, Ely
08600		AV Dawson, Ayrton Rail Terminal, Middlesbrough
08602	004 BOMBER	Bombardier Transportation, Derby Works
08613	H064	Celtic Energy, Onllwyn Coal & Distribution Centre, West Glamorgan
08622	H028 19	Hanson Cement, Ketton Cement Works, Stamford
08629	Bradwell	Railcare, Wolverton Works, Milton Keynes
08643		Bardon Aggregates, Merehead Stone Terminal
08648	OLD GEOFF 20	PD Ports, Teesport, Grangetown, Middlesbrough
08649	Wolverton	Railcare, Wolverton Works, Milton Keynes
08650	ISLE OF GRAIN	Knights Rail Services, Eastleigh Works
08652		Hanson Aggregates, Whatley Quarry, near Frome
08670		Colne Valley Railway, Halstead, Essex
08678	ARTILA	West Coast Railway Company, Carnforth
08682	D3849 Lionheart	Bombardier Transportation, Derby Works
08683		Colne Valley Railway, Halstead, Essex
08685		Barrow Hill Roundhouse, Chesterfield
08697		RVEL, RTC Business Park, Derby
08699		Tata Steel, Shotton Works, Deeside, Flintshire
08704	D3871	East Lancashire Railway, Bury, Greater Manchester
08730	The Caley	Railcare, Springburn Depot, Glasgow
08743	Bryan Turner	SembCorp Utilities Teesside, Wilton, Middlesbrough
08750		Weardale Railway, Wolsingham, County Durham
08754		Wabtec Rail Scotland, Caledonian Works, Kilmarnock
08756		Tata Steel, Shotton Works, Deeside, Flintshire
08762		Cemex UK, Washwood Heath, Birmingham
08764		Maritime Transport, Tilbury Railport, Tilbury
08765		Nemesis Rail, Burton-upon-Trent, Staffordshire
08774	ARTHUR VERNON DAWSON	AV Dawson, Ayrton Rail Terminal, Middlesbrough
08786		Barrow Hill Roundhouse, Chesterfield, Derbyshire
08787	08296	Hanson Aggregates, Machen Quarry, nr Newport
08807		AV Dawson, Ayrton Rail Terminal, Middlesbrough
08809		Hanson Traction, Washwood Heath, Birmingham
08810		Northern, Heaton Depot, Newcastle
08818	MOLLY	Flixborough Wharf, Flixborough, Scunthorpe
08823	LIBBIE	Daventry International Railfreight Terminal, Crick
08834		Bombardier Transportation, Old Dalby Test Centre, Asfordby
08846	003	Bombardier Transportation, Derby Works
08868		LNWR, Crewe Carriage Depot, Crewe, Cheshire
08870	H024	Weardale Railway, Wolsingham, County Durham
08871	22	Weardale Railway, Wolsingham, County Durham
08885	H042 18	PD Ports, Teesport, Grangetown, Middlesbrough
08892		Nemesis Rail, Burton-upon-Trent, Staffordshire
08903	JOHN W. ANTILL	SembCorp Utilities Teesside, Wilton, Middlesbrough

08905		Lafarge Cement, Blue Circle Cement Works, Hope, Derbyshire
08912		AV Dawson, Ayrton Rail Terminal, Middlesbrough
08913		Daventry International Railfreight Terminal, Crick
08918		Nemesis Rail, Burton-upon-Trent, Staffordshire
08924		Barrow Hill Roundhouse, Chesterfield, Derbyshire
08933		Bardon Aggregates, Merehead Stone Terminal
08936		Tata Steel, Shotton Works, Deeside, Flintshire
08937	BLUEBELL MEL	Bardon Aggregates, Meldon Quarry, Okehampton
08943		Bombardier Transportation, Central Rivers Depot, Barton-under-Needwood
08947		Bardon Aggregates, Isle of Grain, Kent
08954		Nemesis Rail, Burton-upon-Trent, Staffordshire
08956		Bombardier Transportation, Old Dalby Test Centre, Asfordby

Class 09

09007	D3671	London Overground, Willesden Depot, London
09012	Dick Hardy	Barrow Hill Roundhouse, Chesterfield, Derbyshire
09014		Nemesis Rail, Burton-upon-Trent, Staffordshire
09018		Lafarge Cement, Blue Circle Cement Works, Hope, Derbyshire
09019		Nemesis Rail, Burton-upon-Trent, Staffordshire
09022		Victoria Group, Port of Boston, Boston
09204		LNWR, Crewe Carriage Depot, Crewe, Cheshire

Class 14

D9504		Kent & East Sussex Railway
D9529	14029	Nene Valley Railway

Class 20

20056	81	Tata Steel, Appleby-Frodingham Works, Scunthorpe
20066	82	Tata Steel, Appleby-Frodingham Works, Scunthorpe
20168	SIR GEORGE EARLE	Lafarge Cement, Blue Circle Cement Works, Hope, Derbyshire

Class 47

47714		Bombardier Transportation, Old Dalby Test Centre, Asfordby

Class 56

56009	56201	Brush Traction, Loughborough Works

5. LOCOMOTIVES AWAITING DISPOSAL

Locomotives that are still extant but at scrapyards are listed here.

Class 08

08646	F	European Metal Recycling, Kingsbury
08662	E	TJ Thomson, Stockton
08745	FE	CF Booth, Rotherham
08783	E	European Metal Recycling, Kingsbury
08798	E	European Metal Recycling, Attercliffe
08872	E	European Metal Recycling, Attercliffe
08921	E	European Metal Recycling, Kingsbury

Class 09

09023	E	European Metal Recycling, Kingsbury
09107	E	European Metal Recycling, Kingsbury
09205	DG	TJ Thomson, Stockton

Class 56

56031	FER	European Metal Recycling, Kingsbury
56032	FER	European Metal Recycling, Kingsbury
56038	FER	European Metal Recycling, Kingsbury
56049	FER	European Metal Recycling, Kingsbury
56069	FER	European Metal Recycling, Kingsbury
56074	FER	European Metal Recycling, Kingsbury
56104	FER	European Metal Recycling, Kingsbury
56106	FER	European Metal Recycling, Kingsbury

6. LOCOMOTIVES EXPORTED FOR USE ABROAD

This section details former BR (plus privatisation era) diesel and electric locomotives that have been exported from the UK for use in industrial locations or by a main line operator abroad. Not included are locos that are "preserved" abroad, which are included in our "Preserved Locomotives" publication. Generally locos are included here if they are expected to remain abroad for more than one year.

Number Other no./name   Location

Class 04

D2289		Lonato SpA, Lonato Steelworks, Lonato, Brescia, Italy

Class 56

56101	0659 001-5	FLOYD, Hungary
56115	0659 002-3	FLOYD, Hungary

Class 58

58001		Axiom Rail, Alizay, France (stored)
58004		Axiom Rail, Alizay, France (stored)
58005		Axiom Rail, Alizay, France (stored)
58006		Axiom Rail, Alizay, France (stored)
58007		Axiom Rail, Alizay, France (stored)
58009		Axiom Rail, Alizay, France (stored)
58010		Axiom Rail, Alizay, France (stored)
58011		Axiom Rail, Alizay, France (stored)
58013		Axiom Rail, Alizay, France (stored)
58015	L54	Transfesa, Spain
58018		Axiom Rail, Alizay, France (stored)
58020	L43	Transfesa, Spain
58021		Axiom Rail, Alizay, France (stored)
58024	L42	Transfesa, Spain
58025	L41	Continental Rail, Spain (stored)
58026		Axiom Rail, Alizay, France (stored)
58027	L52	Continental Rail, Spain (stored)
58029	L44	Transfesa, Spain
58030	L46	Transfesa, Spain
58031	L45	Transfesa, Spain
58032		Axiom Rail, Alizay, France (stored)
58033		Axiom Rail, Alizay, France (stored)
58034		Axiom Rail, Alizay, France (stored)
58035		Axiom Rail, Alizay, France (stored)
58036		Axiom Rail, Alizay, France (stored)
58038		Axiom Rail, Alizay, France (stored)
58039		Axiom Rail, Alizay, France (stored)
58040		Axiom Rail, Alizay, France (stored)
58041	L36	Transfesa, Spain
58042		Axiom Rail, Alizay, France (stored)
58043	L37	Transfesa, Spain
58044		Axiom Rail, Alizay, France (stored)
58046		Axiom Rail, Alizay, France (stored)
58047	L51	Transfesa, Spain
58049		Axiom Rail, Alizay, France (stored)
58050	L53	Continental Rail, Spain (stored)

Class 59

59003	YEOMAN HIGHLANDER	
	259 003-2	Heavy Haul Power International, Germany

Class 66

66022	Euro Cargo Rail, France
66026	Euro Cargo Rail, France
66028	Euro Cargo Rail, France
66029	Euro Cargo Rail, France
66032	Euro Cargo Rail, France
66036	Euro Cargo Rail, France
66038	Euro Cargo Rail, France

66049	Euro Cargo Rail, France
66064	Euro Cargo Rail, France
66073	Euro Cargo Rail, France
66146	DB Schenker Rail Polska, Poland
66153	DB Schenker Rail Polska, Poland
66157	DB Schenker Rail Polska, Poland
66159	DB Schenker Rail Polska, Poland
66163	DB Schenker Rail Polska, Poland
66166	DB Schenker Rail Polska, Poland
66173	DB Schenker Rail Polska, Poland
66178	DB Schenker Rail Polska, Poland
66179	Euro Cargo Rail, France
66180	DB Schenker Rail Polska, Poland
66189	DB Schenker Rail Polska, Poland
66190	Euro Cargo Rail, France
66191	Euro Cargo Rail, France
66195	Euro Cargo Rail, France
66196	DB Schenker Rail Polska, Poland
66202	Euro Cargo Rail, France
66203	Euro Cargo Rail, France
66205	Euro Cargo Rail, France
66208	Euro Cargo Rail, France
66209	Euro Cargo Rail, France
66210	Euro Cargo Rail, France
66211	Euro Cargo Rail, France
66212	Euro Cargo Rail, France
66214	Euro Cargo Rail, France
66215	Euro Cargo Rail, France
66216	Euro Cargo Rail, France
66217	Euro Cargo Rail, France
66219	Euro Cargo Rail, France
66220	DB Schenker Rail Polska, Poland
66222	Euro Cargo Rail, France
66224	Euro Cargo Rail, France
66225	Euro Cargo Rail, France
66226	Euro Cargo Rail, France
66227	DB Schenker Rail Polska, Poland
66228	Euro Cargo Rail, France
66229	Euro Cargo Rail, France
66231	Euro Cargo Rail, France
66233	Euro Cargo Rail, France
66234	Euro Cargo Rail, France
66235	Euro Cargo Rail, France
66236	Euro Cargo Rail, France
66237	DB Schenker Rail Polska, Poland
66239	Euro Cargo Rail, France
66240	Euro Cargo Rail, France
66241	Euro Cargo Rail, France
66242	Euro Cargo Rail, France
66243	Euro Cargo Rail, France
66244	Euro Cargo Rail, France

66246		Euro Cargo Rail, France
66247		Euro Cargo Rail, France
66248		DB Schenker Rail Polska, Poland
66411	66013	Freightliner, Poland
66417	66014	Freightliner, Poland
66582	66009	Freightliner, Poland
66583	66010	Freightliner, Poland
66584	66011	Freightliner, Poland
66586	66008	Freightliner, Poland
66608	66603	Freightliner, Poland
66609	66604	Freightliner, Poland
66611	66605	Freightliner, Poland
66612	66606	Freightliner, Poland
66624	66602	Freightliner, Poland
66625	66601	Freightliner, Poland

Class 86

86215	0450 005-8	FLOYD, Hungary
86218	0450 004-1	FLOYD, Hungary
86232	0450 003-3	FLOYD, Hungary
86248	0450 001-7	FLOYD, Hungary
86250	0450 002-5	FLOYD, Hungary

Class 87

87003	87003-0	BZK, Bulgaria
87004	87004-8 Britannia	BZK, Bulgaria
87006	87006-3	BZK, Bulgaria
87007	87007-1	BZK, Bulgaria
87008	87008-9	BZK, Bulgaria (stored)
87010	87010-5	BZK, Bulgaria
87012	87012-1	BZK, Bulgaria
87013	87013-9	BZK, Bulgaria
87014	87014-7	BZK, Bulgaria (stored)
87019	87019-6	BZK, Bulgaria
87020	87020-4	BZK, Bulgaria
87022	87022-0	BZK, Bulgaria
87026	87026-1	BZK, Bulgaria
87028	87028-7	BZK, Bulgaria
87029	87029-5	BZK, Bulgaria
87033	87033-7	BZK, Bulgaria
87034	87034-5	BZK, Bulgaria

Class 92

92034	Kipling	DB Schenker, Bulgaria

Locomotives being prepared for export:

86117	0659 003-1	for FLOYD, Hungary (at Nemesis Rail, Burton)
86217	0450 006-	for FLOYD, Hungary (at Europhoenix, Long Marston)
87017		for Bulmarket, Bulgaria (at Willesden Depot)
87023		for Bulmarket, Bulgaria (at Willesden Depot)

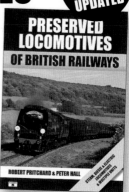

7. CODES

7.1. LIVERY CODES

Livery codes are used to denote the various liveries carried. It is impossible to list every livery variation which currently exists, in particular items ignored for this publication include:

- Minor colour variations.
- Omission of logos.
- All numbering, lettering and brandings.

Descriptions quoted are thus a general guide only. Logos as appropriate for each livery are normally deemed to be carried. The colour of the lower half of the bodyside is stated first..

"One" (metallic grey with a broad black bodyside stripe. White National Express "interim" stripe as branding).
B Arriva Trains Wales "executive" dark & light blue.
AI Aggregate Industries (green, light grey & blue).
AL Advertising/promotional livery (see class heading for details).
R Anglia Railways (turquoise blue with a white stripe).
Z Advenza Freight (deep blue with green Advenza brandings).
BR blue.
L BR Revised blue with yellow cabs, grey roof, large numbers & logo.
D Cotswold Rail (silver with blue & red logo).
E BR Civil Engineers (yellow & grey with black cab doors & window surrounds).
S Colas Rail (yellow, orange & black).
U Corus (silver with red logos).
B DB Schenker (Deutsche Bahn red with grey roof and solebar).
C Devon & Cornwall Railway (dark green).
G BR Departmental (dark grey with black cab doors & window surrounds).
R Direct Rail Services (dark blue with light blue or dark grey roof).
S Revised Direct Rail Services (dark blue, light blue & green. "Compass" logo).
English Welsh & Scottish Railway (maroon bodyside & roof with a broad gold bodyside band).
B Eurotunnel (two-tone grey with a broad blue stripe).
C East Coast (silver or grey with a purple stripe).
CR Euro Cargo Rail (light grey).
G "EWS grey" (as **F** but with large yellow & red EWS logo).
L Electric Traction Limited (silver & red).
P European Passenger Services (two-tone grey with dark blue roof).
X Europhoenix (silver, blue & red).
BR Trainload Freight (two-tone grey with black cab doors & window surrounds. Various logos).
A Fastline Freight (grey & black with white & orange stripes).
B First Group dark blue.
E Railfreight Distribution International (two tone-grey with black cab doors & dark blue roof).
ER Fertis (light grey with a dark grey roof & solebar).

FF	Freightliner grey (two-tone grey with black cab doors & window surrounds. Freightliner logo).
FH	Revised Freightliner {PowerHaul} (dark green with yellow ends & a grey stripe/buffer beam).
FL	Freightliner (dark green with yellow cabs).
FO	BR Railfreight (grey bodysides, yellow cabs & red lower bodyside stripe, large BR logo).
FR	Fragonset Railways (black with silver roof & a red bodyside band lined out in silver).
FS	First Group (indigo blue with pink & white stripes).
FY	Foster Yeoman (blue & silver. Cast numberplates).
G	BR Green (plain green, with white stripe on main line locomotives).
GB	GB Railfreight (blue with orange cantrail & solebar stripes, orange cabs).
GC	Grand Central (all over black with an orange stripe).
GG	BR green (two-tone green).
GIF	GIF (Spain) light blue with a dark blue band.
GL	First Great Western locos (green with a gold stripe (no gold stripe on shunters).
GN	Great North Eastern Railway {modified} (dark blue with white National Express "interim" stripe as branding).
GS	Royal Scotsman maroon.
GV	Gatwick Express EMU (red, white & indigo blue with mauve & blue doors).
GW	Great Western Railway (green, lined out in black & orange).
GX	Gatwick Express InterCity (dark grey/white/burgundy/white).
GY	Eurotunnel (grey & yellow).
HA	Hanson Quarry Products (dark blue/silver with oxide red roof).
HN	Harry Needle Railroad Company (orange with a black roof and solebar).
IC	BR InterCity (dark grey/white/red/white).
K	Black.
LH	BR Loadhaul (black with orange cabsides).
LM	London Midland (white/grey & green with broad black stripe around windows).
M	BR maroon.
MA	Maintrain/East Midlands Trains blue.
ML	BR Mainline Freight (aircraft blue with a silver stripe).
MT	GB Railfreight Metronet (blue with orange cabsides).
N	BR Network SouthEast (white & blue with red lower bodyside stripe, grey solebar & cab ends).
NX	National Express (white with grey ends).
O	Non-standard (see class heading for details).
PC	Pullman Car Company (umber & cream with gold lettering lined out in gold).
RG	BR Parcels (dark grey & red).
RP	Royal Train (claret, lined out in red & black).
RV	Riviera Trains (Oxford blue).
RX	Rail Express Systems (dark grey & red with or without blue markings).
RZ	Royal Train revised (plain claret, no lining).
SD	South West Trains outer suburban {Class 450 style} (deep blue, orange & red).
SL	Silverlink (indigo blue with white stripe, green lower body & yellow doors).
ST	Stagecoach {long-distance stock} (white & dark blue with dark blue window surrounds and red & orange swishes at unit ends).
TT	Transmart Trains (all over green).

U   White or grey undercoat.
V   Virgin Trains (red with black doors extending into bodysides, three white lower bodyside stripes).
VN   Northern Belle (crimson lake & cream lined out in gold).
VP   Virgin Trains shunters (black with a large black & white chequered flag on the bodyside).
VT   Virgin Trains silver (silver with red roof. Red swept down at ends).
WA   Wabtec Rail (black).
WC   West Coast Railway Company maroon.
WS   Wrexham & Shropshire (two-tone grey & silver).
XC   CrossCountry (two-tone grey with deep crimson ends and pink doors).
Y   Network Rail yellow.

7.2. OWNER CODES

Locomotives and rolling stock are owned by various companies and private owners and are allotted codes as follows:

20	Class 20189
40	Class Forty Preservation Society
47	Stratford 47 Group
50	Class 50 Alliance
56	Class 56 Locomotives
70	7029 Clun Castle
71	71A Locomotives
2L	Class Twenty Locomotive Society
A	Angel Trains
AI	Aggregate Industries
AM	Alstom
AV	Arriva UK Trains
BA	British American Railway Services
BN	Beacon Rail Leasing
CS	Colas Rail
DB	DB Schenker Rail (UK)
DP	Deltic Preservation Society
DR	Direct Rail Services
DT	The Diesel Traction Group
E	Eversholt Rail (UK)
ED	Edward Stevenson
EL	Electric Traction Limited
EM	East Midlands Trains
EP	Europhoenix
ET	Eurotunnel
EU	Eurostar (UK)
FG	First Group
FL	Freightliner
FW	First Great Western (assets of the Greater Western franchise)
GB	GB Railfreight
HA	The Hanson Group
HN	Harry Needle Railroad Company
HU	Hunslet Engine Company

IR	Riley & Son (Railways)
LM	London Midland
LY	Lloyds Banking Group
MW	Martin Walker
NM	National Museum of Science & Industry
NR	Network Rail
NS	Nemesis Rail
NY	North Yorkshire Moors Railway Enterprises
P	Porterbrook Leasing Company
PO	Other owner
PP	Peter Pan Locomotive Company
RE	Railway Vehicle Engineering
RL	Rail Management Services (trading as RMS Locotec)
RV	Riviera Trains
SN	Southern
TT	Transmart Trains
WA	Wabtec Rail
WC	West Coast Railway Company
X	Sold for scrap/further use and awaiting collection.
ZW	Zweig

7.3. LOCOMOTIVE POOL CODES

Locomotives are split into operational groups ("pools") for diagramming and maintenance purposes. The official codes used to denote these pools are shown in this publication.

ACAC	Electric Traction Limited locomotives
ACXX	Electric Traction Limited locomotives for static depot use.
ATLO	Alstom Class 08.
ATZZ	Alstom stored locomotives.
CFOL	Class 50 Operations locomotives.
COLO	Colas Rail locomotives.
DFEP	Freightliner locos for export to Poland.
DFGC	Freightliner Intermodal Class 86/5.
DFGH	Freightliner Heavy Haul Class 70.
DFGI	Freightliner Intermodal Class 70.
DFGM	Freightliner Intermodal Class 66.
DFHG	Freightliner Heavy Haul modified Class 66.
DFHH	Freightliner Heavy Haul Class 66.
DFIM	Freightliner Intermodal modified Class 66.
DFIN	Freightliner Intermodal Class 66 (low emission).
DFLC	Freightliner Intermodal Class 90.
DFLH	Freightliner Heavy Haul Class 47.
DFLS	Freightliner Class 08.
DFNC	Freightliner Intermodal Class 86/6.
DFRT	Freightliner Heavy Haul Class 66. Infrastructure services.
DFTZ	Freightliner locomotives (holding pool).
DHLT	Freightliner locomotives awaiting maintenance/repair/disposal.
EFOO	First Great Western Class 57.
EFPC	First Great Western Class 43.

EFSH	First Great Western Class 08.
EHPC	CrossCountry Class 43.
EJLO	London Midland Class 08.
ELRD	East Lancashire Railway-based main line registered locomotives.
EMPC	East Midlands Trains Class 43.
EMSL	East Midlands Trains Class 08.
EPXS	Europhoenix locomotives (stored).
EPXX	Europhoenix Class 56 & 86.
ETLO	Electric Traction Limited Class 86/7.
GBCM	GB Railfreight Class 66. General.
GBED	GB Railfreight Class 73.
GBEE	GB Railfreight Class 20. On hire from Harry Needle/Class 20189.
GBET	GB Railfreight Class 92.
GBFM	GB Railfreight Class 66. RETB fitted.
GBRT	GB Railfreight Class 66. Network Rail duties.
GBSD	GB Railfreight Class 66.
GBWM	GB Railfreight Class 08/09.
GBZZ	GB Railfreight. Stored locomotives.
GCHP	Grand Central Class 43.
GPSS	Eurostar (UK) Class 08.
HBSH	Wabtec hire shunting locomotives.
HNRL	Harry Needle Railroad Company hire locomotives.
HNRS	Harry Needle Railroad Company stored locomotives.
HTLX	British American Railway Services locomotives.
HWSU	Southern Class 09.
HYWD	South West Trains Class 73.
IANA	Greater Anglia Class 90.
IECA	East Coast Class 91.
IECP	East Coast Class 43.
IWCA	Virgin Trains Class 57.
MBDL	Non TOC-owned diesel locomotives.
MBED	Non TOC-owned electro-diesel locomotives.
MBEL	Non TOC-owned electric locomotives.
MRSO	RMS Locotec Class 08.
NRHL	Nemisis Rail hire locomotives.
NRLO	Nemesis Rail locomotives.
PTXX	GB Railfreight Class 92 (stored).
QACL	Network Rail Class 86.
QADD	Network Rail diesel locomotives.
QCAR	Network Rail New Measurement Train Class 43.
QETS	Network Rail Class 37.
RFSH	Wabtec Rail locomotives.
RTLO	Riviera Trains Class 47.
RVLO	Rail Vehicle Engineering locomotives.
SBXL	Porterbrook Leasing Company off-lease locomotives.
WAAN	DB Schenker Class 67.
WABN	DB Schenker Class 67. RETB fitted.
WATN	DB Schenker Class 67 for hire to Arriva Trains Wales.
WAWN	DB Schenker Class 67 for hire to Chiltern Railways.
WBAI	DB Schenker Industrial Class 66.
WBAL	DB Schenker Logistics Class 66.

WBAK	DB Schenker Construction Class 66.
WBBI	DB Schenker Industrial Class 66. RETB fitted.
WBBL	DB Schenker Logistics Class 66. RETB fitted.
WBBK	DB Schenker Construction Class 66. RETB fitted.
WBEN	DB Schenker Class 66. Returned from France
WBES	DB Schenker Class 66. Restricted use.
WBLI	DB Schenker Industrial Class 66. Dedicated locomotives for Lickey Incline banking duties.
WCAI	DB Schenker Industrial Class 60.
WCAK	DB Schenker Construction Class 60.
WCBI	DB Schenker Industrial Class 60. Extended-range fuel tanks.
WCBK	DB Schenker Construction Class 60. Extended-range fuel tanks.
WDAK	DB Schenker Construction Class 59.
WEFE	DB Schenker Class 90.
WFMU	DB Schenker Fleet Management Unit locomotives.
WNSO	DB Schenker locomotives sold awaiting collection.
WNTR	DB Schenker locomotives – short-term maintenance/tactical reserve.
WNTS	DB Schenker locomotives – tactical stored unserviceable.
WNWX	DB Schenker locomotives – on heavy repair or for heavy repair.
WNXX	DB Schenker locomotives – stored unserviceable.
WNYX	DB Schenker Class 08/09 tactical reserve.
WSSI	DB Schenker Industrial operational Shunters.
WSSL	DB Schenker Logistics operational Shunters
WSSK	DB Schenker Construction operational Shunters.
WSXX	DB Schenker shunting locomotives – internal/depot use.
WTAE	DB Schenker Class 92.
WTHE	DB Schenker Class 92 with commissioned TVM430 cab signalling equipment for use on High Speed 1.
WZKS	DB Schenker Class 37. Returned from Spain
XHAC	Direct Rail Services Class 37/4 and 47.
XHCK	Direct Rail Services Class 57.
XHHP	Direct Rail Services locomotives – holding pool.
XHIM	Direct Rail Services locomotives – Intermodal traffic.
XHNC	Direct Rail Services locomotives – nuclear traffic/general.
XHSS	Direct Rail Services stored locomotives.
XYPA	Mendip Rail Class 59/1.
XYPO	Mendip Rail Class 59/0.

7.4. ALLOCATION & LOCATION CODES   * = unofficial code

Allocation codes are used in this publication to denote the normal maintenance base ("depots") of each operational locomotive. However maintenance may be carried out at other locations and also by mobile teams. The designation (S) denotes stored.

Code	Location	Depot Operator
BA	Basford Hall Yard (Crewe)	Freightliner
BH	Barrow Hill (Chesterfield)	Barrow Hill Engine Shed Society
BN	Bounds Green (London)	East Coast
BO	Burton-upon-Trent	Nemesis Rail
BQ	Bury (Greater Manchester)	East Lancashire Rly/Riley & Son Railways
BZ	St Blazey (Par)	*Storage location only*

CD	Crewe Diesel	DB Schenker Rail (UK)
CE	Crewe International	DB Schenker Rail (UK)
CO	Coquelles (France)	Eurotunnel
CP	Crewe Carriage	LNWR (part of Arriva)
CQ	Crewe Heritage Centre	LNWR Heritage Company
CR	Crewe Gresty Bridge	Direct Rail Services
CS	Carnforth	West Coast Railway Company
DL	Dollands Moor	*Storage location only*
EC	Edinburgh Craigentinny	East Coast
EH	Eastleigh	LNWR (part of Arriva)
HT	Heaton (Newcastle)	Northern
KM	Carlisle Kingmoor	Direct Rail Services
KR	Kidderminster	Severn Valley Railway
LA	Laira (Plymouth)	First Great Western
LB	Loughborough Works	Brush Traction
LD	Leeds Midland Road	Freightliner Engineering
LE	Landore (Swansea)	First Great Western
LM	Long Marston (Warwickshire)	Motorail Logistics
LT	Longport (Stoke-on-Trent)	Electro Motive Diesel Services
MA	Manchester Longsight	Alstom
MD	Merehead	Mendip Rail
NC	Norwich Crown Point	Greater Anglia
NL	Neville Hill (Leeds)	East Midlands Trains/Northern
NY	Grosmont (North Yorkshire)	North Yorkshire Moors Railway
OO	Old Oak Common HST	First Great Western
PG	Peterborough	GB Railfreight
RU	Rugby Rail Plant	Colas Rail
SE	St Leonards (Hastings)	St Leonards Railway Engineering
SL	Stewarts Lane (London)	Southern/Orient Express Hotels
SK	Swanwick Junction (Derbyshire)	Midland Railway-Butterley
SU	Selhurst (Croydon)	Southern
TM	Tyseley Locomotive Works	Birmingham Railway Museum
TO	Toton (Nottinghamshire)	DB Schenker Rail (UK)
WB	Wembley (London)	Alstom
WD	Wimbledon (London)	South West Trains
WF	Wansford (Cambridgeshire)	Nene Valley Railway
WH*	Washwood Heath (Birmingham)	Boden Rail Engineering
WN	Willesden (London)	London Overground
WO*	Wolsingham, Weardale Railway	British American Railway Services
YK	National Railway Museum (York)	National Museum of Science & Industry
ZA	RTC Business Park (Derby)	Railway Vehicle Engineering
ZB	Doncaster Works	Wabtec Rail
ZC	Crewe Works	Bombardier Transportation UK
ZD	Derby Works	Bombardier Transportation UK
ZG	Eastleigh Works	Arlington Fleet Services
ZH	Springburn Depot (Glasgow)	Railcare
ZI	Ilford Works	Bombardier Transportation UK
ZJ	Stoke Works	Axiom Rail
ZK	Kilmarnock Works	Wabtec Rail Scotland
ZN	Wolverton Works	Railcare
ZR	York (Holgate Works)	Network Rail

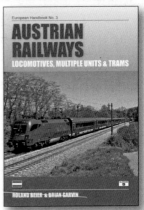